PAMEL

MAKING A DIFFERENCE

Setting up sustainable, community-based projects

Ortus

First published in 2023 by
Ortus Press

A CIP Catalogue of this book is available from
the British Library

ISBN: 978-19113838-3-3

Front cover illustration: melitas/shutterstock.com

Cover design and typeset by
www.chandlerbookdesign.com

Printed in Great Britain by
TJ Books Limited, Padstow, Cornwall

DEDICATION

This book is dedicated to my parents, Claire and Jim, with love and gratitude.

And to my husband, Stephen: Blimey, Carruthers – thirty-four years together!

CONTENTS

INTRODUCTION

*'To make a difference to someone's life, you
don't have to be brilliant, rich, beautiful or
perfect. You just have to care.'* [1]

Your Project is undoubtedly going to make a positive difference
to the lives of many vulnerable people within your Community.
And although the *process* of achieving your goal successfully and
sustainably might seem a little daunting at first, don't worry at all:
you can do it! This book will lead you along the path that you need
to follow, enabling your Project to be shaped and guided by the
Community that you live in and the people that you'll be helping.
And while my thirty years' experience of setting up sustainable
Community-based Projects and managing volunteers leads me to
tell you that it's probably not all going to go smoothly - that's just not
the way the world usually works - you will pick up the tools here
that you need to anticipate, side-step or overcome problems of
any size, both while you're working on setting up your Project, and
when it's established and running. It'll take you from your lightbulb
moment, when you first realised what needed doing within your
Community and how you could help to make that happen, through

to looking around at the useful and productive Project that you will
have begun, alongside your Committee and your volunteers. Take
the time to read through each chapter - and the accompanying
step-by-step illustrative example of establishing a Project that runs
throughout the book - applying your Project idea in a considered
way to every stage. Then, when you're ready, begin.

ENDNOTES

1. Mandy Hale.

1

WHAT DO YOU WANT YOUR PROJECT TO ACHIEVE?

'll just begin by saying that ensuring the dignity of the people benefiting from your service is paramount, and should underpin every aspect of your Project. This is the right thing to do of course – everyone's dignity should be respected – but it is also necessary for the success of your Project: service users* will return repeatedly, and their positive feedback will attract others who could benefit from the service. The number of people attending will encourage organisations to signpost more people to the Project, and will underline the need for the Project to funders. And volunteers will want to support a service in which the self-worth of people is protected and enhanced.

The first question to ask yourself is: What is the *aim* of this Project? That is: who will benefit from it, and in what way? This is very important, because everything that you do subsequently will stem from your answer to this question. Write down an outline of your Project as a first step. This chapter will take you through what to include in this and will encourage you to think about which aspects of your outline are 'set in stone' for you and which are negotiable. It's a starting point that you're preparing for yourself, to keep you focused on what you want your Project to be and to achieve. It'll be amended, revised and tweaked as you go.

Take about 150 words to write your Project idea down, guided by the six sections below:

> **Who** – Who will you be helping?
>
> **What (Outcome)** – What do you hope the Project will achieve? What positive difference do you envisage it will make? For example, alleviating hunger, or loneliness, or increasing play provision for under 5s.
>
> **How** – How will the Project achieve its aims? i.e. How is it going to be delivered? Every aspect of your Project needs to be realistic, based on (initially) limited resources and on your service users' circumstances.
>
> **Why** – Why is this needed, for the service users that you've identified and within the area that you're currently contemplating for delivery of your Project?
>
> **When** – When do you plan to start? Be realistic – it can take several months to get everything in place. And the external groups and organisations that you'll be in touch with won't have your own sense of urgency.
>
> **Where** – You'll need to define the geographical area of your Project - e.g. your local neighbourhood within your town or city.

As you work through the tasks in this book, the chances are that you'll make significant changes to every section, except *who* you'll be helping, and the *outcome* that you want for your service users. These two form the foundation of your Project idea, and are the reason why you're doing this. Changes to some or all of the other four sections are absolutely to be expected, as you begin to gather information on what's currently provided and where, and as you start to see the gaps in services related to your envisaged service users etc. Everything that you will need to inform and guide these changes is set out clearly within this book.

I've given an example here from the early '90s that illustrates how information may change aspects of your Project:

> *I was working to set up free Nursery provision for the children of Gypsies and Travelling families, and envisaged mirroring the work being carried out in other areas – double-decker buses equipped with a teacher and learning resources driving onto various Gypsy and Traveller sites. But after speaking with the Gypsy Council, the parents of the children themselves, local Head Teachers, a children's charity etc., the final plan was for community-based provision that was flexible so that children from the Traveller and Gypsy communities could come and go as their families moved in and out of the area, and which was also integrated with the local Community, providing free Nursery provision too for local children who needed that 'start.'*

So, the '**who**' were the young children of Gypsies and Travellers, and the '**outcome**' was access to Nursery education that was flexible, to allow for the fact that the families of those communities would move in and out of an area every few weeks. As I gathered more information though, it was necessary to make changes to almost every other aspect: **where** – the location of the nursery provision changed from buses on traveller sites to a donated porta cabin on a school playground, in an area of high deprivation; **how** – the community-based provision for the young children of Gypsies and Travellers was opened up to include some local children too; **why** –because affordable nursery provision was in short supply too for many families within the local Community, and the prevailing thinking was to break down the barriers that existed between families in the local Community and in the Gypsy and Traveller Communities. Information will always enhance and enrich your Project. And flexibility (within limits) is a strength.

Think about what the parameters of your Project are for you. How much change would you be comfortable with? What's a definite 'no' for you? Why? People will suggest refinements or even a completely different Project. You need to maintain focus on what you want this Project to achieve. And you need to make sure that you're comfortable with any changes.

JO'S STORY

Jo lives in Tall Town, in the Borough of Sunvale. She writes: I know there are children in my town who go to bed hungry, or have no breakfast, and my son tells me that some of his classmates come to school with just bread and margarine or a bag of crisps for their lunch. I know that many local parents skip meals to feed their children. I would like to provide hot meals for families who cannot afford to eat regularly or healthily, alleviating hunger and adding to health and well-being. I think that takeaway meals would be best – which people could heat up and enjoy in their own homes – and I want these to be free. I'd like to run the service twice a week in term time, and every weekday in the holidays. I think that the need is probably greatest in the north of the town. I expect I could get this started within two months. (150 words)

ENDNOTES

* There are many ways to refer to the group of people that you're aiming to help: 'clients', 'customers' and 'guests' spring to mind. I haven't found the perfect one, so I will be referring to people who could benefit from your Project as 'service users'. It's a cover-all really. Think about how you would like to refer to the people who will benefit from your Project and which title sounds most appropriate for your service, e.g. the term 'guests' might be most appropriate for a meals' service, while 'customers' might be preferred by people accessing school uniform swaps etc.

2

INITIAL INFORMATION-GATHERING

So, you've sketched out your Project, addressing the six sections outlined in the previous chapter. The next step is to find out where there is unmet need related to your Project in your town or city because, whatever issue your Project will be addressing, you need to be able to justify that it is needed in that area, and show the positive impact that it will have for a 'good number' of people. Basically a 'good number' equates to enough people to justify the time, money and other resources invested in the Project, though I appreciate that sounds harsh – because surely just one person helped is worth any amount of resources. However, funders will, of necessity, be pragmatic. It wouldn't be possible to indicate an 'ideal number' of attendees for your Project – it will depend on the service that you're providing and the needs of the people that your Project will be supporting. For example, the older persons' charity, Re-engage, organises intergenerational get-togethers in volunteers' homes, which each include up to ten isolated older people. That could be in a town or city with many thousands of isolated older people living alone and seeing no-one from week to week, but it is recognised that small gatherings in family surroundings, where isolated older people can gradually rebuild their social confidence and chat with new friends over tea and cake, is an ideal environment for that particular need. Southampton City Mission's Clothes Bank opens once a week, and on average provides clothes for thirty-nine people – both adults and children – each time; and at one of the centres of the Swindon Food Collective on just one typical day last year, volunteers provided food, household products and toiletries to help forty-one adults and twenty-nine children, as well as feeding family pets. Ultimately the number of people utilising your Project may only be limited by finite resources, or venue capacity. It will be a smaller number at the outset of your Project, and there may be seasonal fluctuations too – for example, if your Project supports older people, challenging health needs may mean that some cannot utilise your service as much over the winter.

This chapter will take you through what is involved in your initial information-gathering (which is all 'research' is), and will guide you through how to find the information that you need to carry this out. If you already know a couple of like-minded people prepared to help you with this, do share the work. You will need to monitor progress though, because if this research is not comprehensive there will be gaps in your information that might have an impact on the success of your Project.

It's worth noting here that any research needs to be tempered with common sense – which is, as always, your friend. So, for example, you wouldn't need to find out whether the majority of people who are rough sleepers would prefer a safe place that they could call home, or whether lonely older people would like to socialise regularly:

I was once at a meeting hosted by an organisation that had been given thousands of pounds to distribute – in parcels of £2000 – to local Community groups to 'find out what isolated and lonely older people want'. Really? It's not rocket science. Older people want fun like everyone else – good company of all ages, the chance to talk and have a good laugh. Those £2000 grants could really have got the party started.

What will your Research tell you?

Crucially, your research will enable you to answer three questions:

- Is there a *need* for the Project?

- Will it have the support from the Community and from funders that will be essential to making it practical and *sustainable*?

- Will it be filling a gap in current provision, or just be *duplicating* existing work?

There are two main aspects of your initial research which, between them, will answer the questions above:

- The need within the local area that you've chosen for your Project

- The relevant services already being provided by the groups and organisations represented within that area and within the wider town or city.

We'll look at how to carry out this research in this chapter. Taken together, the results will also provide information and insights into the unmet needs of the people who would be accessing your service. And we'll also talk about speaking directly with potential service users later on in this chapter.

Within which area should you base your Project?

What locality have you identified as the focus for your Project? It could be a sprawling urban area, a leafy suburban commuter town, or anything in between. Be led by the research in deciding what area of your town or city to establish your Project in – you'll want to make a significant difference to the lives of as many people as possible. It will certainly need to be a large enough area to be a good source of service users and of volunteers. Look at transport links too, and ask yourself if public transport to your Project is going to be a problem for service users or volunteers within the area you've identified, either because of availability or cost.

There is research available for every neighbourhood within a town or city, and this will allow you to understand where the highest levels of need are in relation to your Project's services: the Government's 'Indices of Multiple Deprivation' [1] is usually a useful starting point. This will have measured deprivation in your immediate area across seven indicators – Income, Employment, Education, Health, Crime, Barriers to Housing & Services (physical and financial), and Living Environment (indoor and outdoor locally) – and compared it to that experienced by the rest of your Local Authority and the rest of the country for a 'relative' score. Some councils will have summarised these findings on their respective websites too. The UK's Office for National Statistics can be a wealth of useful knowledge for your local area on everything from crime and drug use, to education and well-being, to household finances. An internet search too is likely to point to reputable sources of information for any issue for your service users e.g. *I typed in 'hotspots of loneliness in the UK' and found that Age UK had created a map indicating the projected numbers of lonely older people at a neighbourhood level.*

It's possible that not all research avenues will be relevant to your Project: so, for example, for a Project aimed at alleviating the loneliness of isolated older people, your focus would be on demonstrating the levels of loneliness experienced by this group in the area, and the benefits of company in terms of health and wellbeing. If your Project aims to provide free or low cost meals for struggling families, you'd want to research the numbers of households on low incomes in the area, the proportion of local children in poverty, etc.

How do you find these local groups and organisations?

Local groups and organisations relevant to your proposed Project – i.e. providing a related service and/or supporting the same service users – will be invaluable in allowing you to build a picture of existing provision in your town or city. This will ensure that you are not duplicating services and that your Project will be based in an area of currently unmet need. There are a number of sources of information to enable you to identify these relevant local groups and organisations:

Your local Directory of Services

Look at the respective websites of the local CVS* (Council for Voluntary Services) and the City Council. On those sites you're looking for their Directory of Services, a database that will include the organisations and groups working to support your envisaged client group, outlining their work and providing contact details and a link to their respective websites. You can usually search the CVS or Council Directories using key words, but you might miss something so, unless it's obviously an irrelevant section (e.g. related to adults when your envisaged Project is exclusively for children), just plough through it. You'll be noting:

- The names of the groups and any contact details

- How they work – e.g. is it volunteer-led? Does it operate every weekday afternoon? etc.

- Who benefits from this work and in what way

- What their delivery 'looks like' – e.g. if it's free food provision, is that a communal hot meals service, or maybe a foodbank? If it's a social club for older people, does it include free tea and biscuits or a subsidised two course lunch?

- What geographical area they cover.

Check that any internet links are still operational. If there's a link to an organisation's website but it's no longer 'live', do a quick internet search to see if it's still operating.

Occasionally you'll find that neither your council nor the local CVS maintains an online directory. In that case, don't worry. You'll want to register to join your local CVS anyway – it's free, and they are a wealth of useful information and will facilitate most useful local networks. And if they are the sole gatekeepers for the information that you need, then that's just something to include when you explain what you're doing and what you'd like from them.

Your local Council – Contact the council to speak with the person representing your area of interest: if you're setting up not-for-profit food provision you'll want to speak with their Food Insecurity Manager, or Community Engagement Officer, or similar. Or if you're going to be supporting isolated older people, it'd usually be the person representing Adult Social Care initially. For Projects supporting rough sleepers and the vulnerably housed, it'd be your council's Homeless Unit. And if you plan to help people who have substance misuse issues, you'd want to speak with the council's Health Improvement Officer. For Projects providing opportunities for children to play, it'd be your council's Early Years Officer, etc. If you're unsure, just speak with the reception staff at the council offices – they will have a directory of employees and their roles. The appropriate member of council staff will be able to introduce you to local groups and organisations relevant to your Project, and invite you to a local networking meeting. Some council employees can be more difficult to track down than others, and you could always ask your Ward Councillor for an introduction (you are, after all, a resident).

The local council may also have a '**Livewell team**', which will be aware of local forums and networks focused on 'Health and Wellbeing' – everything from help in stopping smoking and reducing alcohol consumption, to healthy eating, to living with long-term health conditions – and they should know what is being delivered related to their focus, by who, and where. This team would be a further way to access relevant forums and networks.

What information could local groups and organisations tell you?

This initial research will enable you to identify a number of areas of need within your town or city – i.e. areas in which your research tells you there are potential service users that your Project could support – and to find out what services are already running in that area, so that you can identify whether there is *unmet* need. The relevant local groups and organisations serving the area should be a wealth of information of the 'who, what, when, where and how' variety. (Chapter 5 – on Communication – will outline how you might want to approach these groups and organisations.) Basically, you need to learn:

- Where existing services are delivered from (if there are any)

- What these services 'look like' (e.g. if it's food provision, is it free / 'pay what you can' etc? and whether the provision is hot meals or bags of ingredients, sandwiches or soup…)

- How often the services run?

- And at what time of day?

- How many service users typically attend?

- What barriers to this attendance have been identified, if any?

- Have any problems been identified in the delivery of the Project?

- Is there a referral system, or is it direct access?

In addition, **relevant organisations may have carried out (or commissioned) research** nationally or regionally that would be useful to you. Summaries are often on these organisations' websites, but if not they are often willing to share it if asked. **Read the annual reports** of any organisations that you're interested in too.** You will learn where they are in their 3 or 5 Year Plan, what they've achieved, what they're currently working on and what they plan to tackle next. These organisations could provide you with information and introduce you to relevant contacts, and they will be keen to speak with you if you can help them to achieve their targets in any way – e.g. staff will be aware that helping you will be kindly looked upon by their funders, and should ultimately give them another option to signpost their service users to.

Further sources of information

Local Faith groups would be well worth contacting, just to find out about the community services that they run and whether their provision or their plans mirror yours. (They may well be aware of other local services that might be relevant to your Project, too.) And when your Project is up and running, these groups will be able to signpost service users to your Project, and vice versa, so it's good to start that relationship now.

Your local Councillors will have some knowledge of local services – planned, running currently or recently closed – and can also help provide introductions to relevant organisations, networks and individuals. N.B. Just check the political affiliations of your councillors before approaching them. (That information is on every council's website.) There may, rarely, be some outside the mainstream that you won't want your Project associated with.

An internet search will be invaluable in providing information on current initiatives around your Project idea. For example, I typed in 'Councils and Play Provision' and came across: 'Play England', an organisation that works to promote the importance of play, working with frontline providers and providing expert information nationally and internationally[2]; the publication 'Best Playbook'[3], produced through a partnership between the National Playing Fields Association, PLAYLINK and the Children's Play Council; and the information that UNICEF is working with Councils across the UK to create Child-Friendly Cities & Communities[4]. Just get hold of a thread and follow it! (Making a note of each internet link as you go.)

A **Local, Parish or Town Council** – though these only cover 30% of England. They are the first tier of local government. They have elected councillors, and 'work towards improving community well-being and providing better services'[5]. They may have some relevant contacts for you, not least for the local organisations that hire rooms in their Community Centres. You could contact them via the National Association of Local Councils, or through their individual websites. (Local Councils are also mentioned in the chapter on fundraising, as they are a grant-giving body too.)

The sum of all this research will enable you to build a 'map' of existing provision serving the area, that's related to your service users and to the way that you see your service being delivered. Through this you can identify gaps in provision, or 'areas of unmet need'. And it will enable you to learn from the successes and mistakes of others in the delivery of your Project.

Speaking with potential service users

The initial information-gathering already outlined in this chapter would be sufficient to broadly understand many of the needs of your potential service users, and there may be no other productive research options for you at this stage: for example, people with substance misuse issues, or the vulnerably housed, would be very difficult to access and usefully speak with directly unless you work within an organisation providing direct support for these service users. It might be, though, that you're already in touch with the people who could benefit from your planned service. For example, maybe you're a parent wanting to set up a uniform / clothes swap with other parents, or a volunteer already supporting isolated older people in the community. If you are already in touch with your potential service users, then you'll probably want to supplement any existing research with a show of hands (one example of a 'straw poll') on one or two broadly encompassing questions – e.g. 'Who fancies a Gateaux and Gossip group?' Or perhaps you might want to compile a short survey based around the specific Project that you're envisaging, as an additional avenue of research. I'll cover surveys more fully in the chapter on Monitoring and Evaluation (chapter 12), because if you don't need them now – though who doesn't love a good survey? – you will certainly need them to ensure the sustainability of your Project when it's up and running.

For now though, should you have the opportunity to carry out a short survey, here's a quick overview:

A survey is basically just a list of questions, the answers to which will provide insight into the particular topic that you're interested in. At this initial stage the answers should tell you: what is attractive about your planned Project from the viewpoint of potential service users, where the weaknesses are, and what you might like to build in – or keep a mental note of for the future growth of your Project. It would be best to ask no more than six or eight straightforward questions really, in order to hold the interest of the people taking part.

How to frame your survey questions

These surveys should be made up of 'open' questions such as 'What would you like to see from a new service?' 'What do you think you would benefit from?' 'What time of day would be best for you, and why?' and more measurable information such as 'How many hot meals do you eat in a typical week?' Don't be too specific – if your Project idea is, for example, to provide hot meals for rough sleepers every Sunday, you already know the answer to 'Would you like a hot meal every Sunday lunchtime?'

It wouldn't help you to ask 'leading' questions such as 'Wouldn't it be good if...' as people are unlikely to disagree with a question phrased like that, and their answer not only tells you nothing useful, but may be reinforcing an inaccurate assumption of yours.

The information you'll need from your potential service users at this stage:

- What do people like about any existing services?

- How could existing provision be improved upon? What *don't* people like about it?

- What problems are there in accessing these existing services? (Anything from not being on a reliable bus route, to the cost of the service, to the time the service starts...)

- What do service users themselves want to see in terms of provision? i.e. Is there potentially a Project that would add value to the lives of this group of people in a different way?

Surveys do need to take into account the particular needs and circumstances of your envisaged service users, in terms of levels of literacy, visual impairments, etc. So, (depending on any communication issues for the people taking part) it might be best to just read the questions aloud to everyone individually, and to write down responses. And that's much better in terms of response rate than a written survey posted through letterboxes anyway.

Some groups and organisations may be unsupportive or dismissive

This could be for any number of reasons, but it's most likely to be about protecting their funding or their resources. Regrettably, egos can become a factor too – of the 'What do you know? I've been doing this for x number of years and you can't just...' type. Well, do you know what, yes you can! Your research will have identified a gap in provision in that area for your envisaged service users, and you'll have the tools here to enable you to effectively address that need. Don't be put off by suggestions that your Project is already being delivered by them in that area – find out exactly what is being delivered, and how.

> *Example: An organisation once tried to dismiss me by saying that the service that I was working to set up – i.e. free vegetarian hot meals, cooked from scratch and eaten communally – was the same as the day-old reheated meat pies and sausage rolls that they gave out.*

If you can't get clarification from a group – or from their (recently updated) website – about precisely what they deliver, then relevant network facilitators (more on these in chapter 6) and council staff will know what they provide. We'll talk more about contacts, and how you could find out *everything*, in the chapter on communication (chapter 5).

However, it might be that local organisations have already looked into providing your proposed service, within the area that you've identified, but that their research had indicated insufficient need compared to the resources required. And they could assume that you would face the same obstacles. But, while you would naturally want to find out what information they had based their conclusions on, remember that something that isn't viable for an organisation with significant 'core costs' (such as salaries) might be more realistic for a local volunteer-led group.

Duplication of Services

Issues *would* arise if your Project would genuinely be duplicating services already running in the same area. By that I mean for example setting up a community pantry within an area already well served with these, or a second school uniform swap group for a local school. It isn't necessarily duplication though if you'd be running a Project on a different day to an existing service, e.g. a social group for older people or young parents, or a playgroup, or providing a hot meal on a different day to existing provision – people of all ages need multiple opportunities to socialise, and to eat every day. *I know of a woman who walks for up to an hour each way five times a week so that she can eat a free hot meal and pick up some free vegetables and fruit, each from a different local Project every day, which means that she doesn't have to spend her severely limited resources on feeding herself and is able to feed her children healthily when they get home from school.*

Duplicating (as opposed to enhancing) provision would create some problems:

- *You are diluting the pool of available volunteers* (individuals' free time is finite, and your potential volunteers are likely to already be committed elsewhere).

- *Resources for your service users are not being significantly increased.*

- *Your Project won't receive funding.* Only one of you will get funding and, for that to be someone other than the group already delivering it, they will have had to have done something quite flagrantly and demonstrably awful.

- *You won't be a comfortable fit for existing providers.* It's quite frustrating and potentially damaging to existing services just to plonk yourself down and start something, regardless of what's going on around you. You need to be a comfortable fit: e.g. *at the height of the pandemic, a great deal of*

*community-based food provision sprang up overnight, with
(on the whole) well-meaning people taking food donations
and surplus food from kindly individuals and from large supermarkets etc and redistributing them to those in food poverty.
Unfortunately, services were often duplicated, and in some
areas the organisations and community groups that had been
relying on the food donations to support local people saw their
supply dry up. Stocks of supplies in some Foodbanks dropped
to an alarming level etc. Resources are finite.*

If your proposed Project *would* be a duplication of existing provision
in the area, rather than a useful addition, you could instead think
about alternative ways that you could achieve your ends. For
example, if a local organisation is already helping with the provision
of hot meals to low-income families, and that's your Project idea,
maybe that's needed in a different area? Or the same local families
also need a community fridge, or a summer play scheme? ... The
world is your oyster.

Recording your research

It's worth noting here that from the get-go you should make a note
of all your research, including sources, and similarly record the gist
of all your communications (i.e. date, name and title of the person
that you spoke with, and their work contact details, the organisation,
and a summary of what was said). Note both blind-alleys and useful
research avenues for two reasons: so that you don't waste time
repeating fruitless actions; and because, as your Project idea evolves,
something that initially was not relevant may become so. Think about
how this record-keeping would work best for you – there's going
to be an element of trial and error. I keep all my notes as a physical
copy and electronically (just in case – belt and braces!), and I write a
quick progress update every fortnight. This allows me to gauge what
headway's been made, and spot any gaps or areas I've neglected.

Finally, 'research' doesn't end until your Project does.

When your Project is up and running, research will be referred to as 'Monitoring and Evaluation' and that'll be ongoing. We'll talk more about that in chapter 12.

JO'S STORY

Jo looked at the Government's Indices of Deprivation for Tall Town. She found that the town has high levels of deprivation, ranking 16th out of the 317 districts in England, and that there are three areas of most concern in the town – Biddlevale and Tymbown to the North, and Trulegate which is close to the town centre. All three areas rank amongst the 10% most deprived in the country across all measures: Income; Employment; Health and Disability; Education, Skills and Training; Barriers to Housing and Services; Crime; and Living Environment.

On the Council's website, Jo found that all three areas also fall within the 10% most deprived in the country for Income Deprivation affecting Children. Over 65% of the children in the town live in families that receive financial support from the Government. This financial support is predominantly to supplement low incomes, but also to support non-working households. In Trulegate and Tymbown, low-income for families is predominantly because of low-paid work rather than people being unable to work, but in Biddlevale more than half of children live in non-working families. A further 10% of children living in the town are in low-income families that are excluded from receiving benefits because of their immigration status (i.e. having No Recourse to Public Funds). Including the children of these families, around 70% of children in all three areas are eligible for free school meals. It is not known how many fall just outside the parameters for this, though it is believed to be a high number for all three areas.

Jo knew that identifying the town's not-for-profit food providers was the next step. The Council's Directory of Services provided a comprehensive list of these, including those run by local Faith groups, and it gave Jo a good indication of what was currently being provided, and where. Jo noted that there did not appear to be a free meals service for families in the town. Jo did not contact any of the food providers at this stage, as she wanted introductions to these to be predominantly via the appropriate network, or through introductions by established organisations, rather than through cold-calling. She knew that otherwise these largely volunteer-led groups might not give her efforts at reaching out too much of their limited time. Jo learned that the Council did not employ a Food Insecurity Officer, and decided to contact Tall Town CVS to find out who was taking the lead on not-for-profit food-related services in the town.

ENDNOTES

* I'll be using 'CVS' throughout this book, though it could be VSC (Voluntary Sector Council), '[name of city / town] Community Action', 'Voluntary Action [name of city / town]' or similar. But in your internet search, if you type in '[city / town] CVS' you should find it.

** You should also make a note of the funders that are acknowledged in these Annual Reports, as their areas of interest will relate to your Project.

1. The Government's 'Indices of Multiple Deprivation' (IMD) will give you statistics at a neighbourhood level, relative to the rest of the Local Authority District and the rest of the country. The Index of Multiple Deprivation (IMD) is the official measure of relative deprivation in England... People may be considered to be living 'in poverty' if they lack the financial resources to meet their needs, whereas people can be regarded as 'deprived' if they lack any kind of resources, not just income. Ministry of Housing, Communities and Local Government. Statistical release 26th Sept., 2019.

2. https://www.playengland.org.uk/

3. http://www.freeplaynetwork.org.uk/pubs/bestplay.pdf

4. Unicef.org.uk

5. National Association of Local Councils (NALC)

3

SETTING UP AND CHAIRING A COMMITTEE

*'Never doubt that a small group of thoughtful,
committed citizens can change the world;
indeed, it is the only thing that ever has'* [1].

You've identified a specific group of people that you want to help, and the area that your Project would usefully be based in. You have an idea of how your Project will be delivered in practice, and what it will achieve. Now's the time to set up your 'committee'. This quite formal structure – with a designated Chairperson to manage meetings, and established procedures to follow – will need to replace any existing, ad hoc arrangement that you might have, whereby people you know have been pitching in and cooperating to move the Project plan forward. Perhaps the best reason for this – apart from everything you already know about how people behave in unstructured groups – is that you need a mechanism for keeping track of the work, so that you can make sure it's moving in the right direction, and that the tasks being carried out by group members fit their particular personalities and skills set. Also, you'll need to be a properly constituted committee before you can access funding etc. But we'll cover that later on.

A well-chosen and well-run committee will add considerable value – widening the range of ideas, solutions, choices etc. And this chapter includes a little guidance on making sure that your committee *is* well-run – i.e. that it remains focused and relevant, and ultimately achieves the goals of your Project. Some members of your committee may have 'lived experience' of the issue that your Project will be addressing. Having an 'expert by experience' on your committee is valued by funders so, if they don't mind you flagging it up, do so when the time comes!

The committee's initial goal is to reach genuine consensus on the vital points of the Project – i.e. the 'who' and 'what': apart from anything else, everyone will be behind it if they feel part of the decision-making process. And, as a committee, you need to present a united front[2], publicly supporting and respecting the decisions agreed by the majority. Then the more practical work begins, with sharing out tasks to achieve this plan. And in every conversation, discussion group, and meeting, keep asking yourself – 'Does this take us closer to or further away from the goal of setting up the Project?'

Finding Committee Members

You could set up a Facebook page that you'll be able to direct people to. If that's not something you've done before, one of your family or friends will probably know how to do this. If you'd prefer though, you could just carry out an internet search 'setting up a Facebook page' and you'll be guided through the process. Begin your Facebook page with an attention-grabbing headline, as you will with the recruitment of your Project's volunteers later on – for example, if you're planning a literacy Project: 'One in every six adults in England would struggle to read this. You can help us to change that.' Then briefly outline what your Project will involve, and how local people could help to achieve the Project's aims, making a positive difference in their own neighbourhood. Include your preferred email / mobile 'phone number for enquirers. Then talk to local friends and relatives, neighbours and interested colleagues, as well as people from any groups that you attend – gym, dog walking group, book group etc. If you can't generate any interest, it's probably just not a match for their own areas of interest, or their time is already over-committed elsewhere – don't worry. You'll just need to widen the net. Your Ward Councillors might put something in their newsletter (their contact details will be on the Council's website). You could put some information on your local neighbourhood website, and the intranet at work. You could advertise it as a volunteering role at your local CVS or Volunteer Centre... There will be people within your community who are aware of the need, and they're just waiting for someone like you to galvanise everyone into action. And a friend of mine in advertising tells me that people may need to see something up to six times before they act on it. Keep going! As Confucius said: 'Virtue is not left to stand alone'.

The make-up of the Committee

About eight or nine people is usually a good number to make up a committee: too few people and everyone has too many tasks, and too many and it can become unwieldy. Ideally, your committee members will fill the gaps in your knowledge and experience, and they will certainly need to be similarly committed to achieving the aims of your Project. There are three over-arching roles within a committee that need to be filled: Chair, Secretary and Treasurer. I'll outline all three roles here. Be upfront about what each role involves, because misrepresentation is no way to lead a team, and reliable people are needed who have the time and capabilities to fulfil these demanding and responsible roles properly.

Chair – this would preferably be your role, otherwise you might find it difficult if someone else holds this position and your Project subsequently starts going in a direction that you feel would be a mistake. You'll need to keep everyone focused and on track. Just be the Captain of your own ship. A word of caution here though – steering a committee made up of volunteers requires more person-centred skills than you might feel should be utilised when managing a team of staff: a bit more tolerance and understanding is required than you'd see in a typical workplace, but should be tempered with your determination to get this Project up and running successfully.

You will need to:

- be reasonable and even-tempered, open-minded, patient and fair.

- listen to opinions, recognising, valuing and, where practical and relevant, incorporating useful ideas and suggestions.

- explain your reasons for e.g. rejecting impractical ideas, and for reassigning tasks that don't fit that individual's particular skills, while trying to minimise hurt feelings.

- show gratitude for your fellow volunteers' time and efforts – they are invaluable. Unless they aren't, when you may ultimately have to take steps to remove them from the committee…

All this while maintaining focus on achieving the aims of your Project. Nobody said it would be easy, but if you start out with the right team, you're halfway there!

Treehouse designed by a Committee

I saw this pictured in the late 1980s, and it remains relevant today: there is a danger that any group of people can get bogged down in differing views and opinions, trivialities, vested interests, etc. And that would significantly affect the progress of your Project, and indeed whether it even happens at all, let alone whether it embodies your original ideas. But it doesn't have to be like that. As Chair, you will be able to 'steer' the committee in three main ways:

- Through the selection of members by their commitment to the ideals inherent in the Project, and their suitability and relevance to the Project's goals – ideally their skills and experiences will complement and supplement your own, and those of other committee members.

- Through closely monitoring discussions – to prevent meetings from getting a bit out of hand.

- Through the content of each agenda, which is set by the Chair: keeping everyone on track starts with the minutes of the previous agenda, circulated at least a couple of days prior to the meeting, along with the new agenda. Delivering a quick summary reminds people of decisions made, and what tasks were handed out to whom. (Check with the committee members themselves beforehand as to whether they've carried out their agreed tasks, to save wasting time in the meeting.) The agenda will reflect the objectives of the meeting, itemised as discussion and feedback sections. Give timings for each section, and stick to them. (If it's a popular topic then summarise where the group has got to and say you'll devote further time to it at the next meeting.) Make sure that you have given everyone the opportunity to give an opinion – though that might mean politely interrupting someone who's rather long-winded, and summarising their argument to give others the floor (i.e. 'So, what you're saying is...'). Assure everyone that all opinions on the subject under discussion are valid. Knowing this, group members will tend to be more supportive of any decision reached.

Many people struggle to communicate what they want to say clearly, especially in front of a group, so you may need to clarify as well as facilitate:

For example, 'So, Bob, am I right in saying that your argument is ...?' The argument will be reinforced in the minutes then too.

Crucially, the role of Chair is key to ensuring that your Project runs successfully, and that it achieves the aims of your lightbulb moment.

Secretary – Most people have very little idea of the depth and range of this role, or the fundamental part that the post-holder plays in the efficient administration of any committee. There are two main aspects to the role: the well-known (and indispensable) role in record-keeping and disseminating information, and the equally important role of working with all the committee members to ensure that the requirements of the group's Regulator are fulfilled – i.e. either the Charity Commission, the UK Government's Office of the Regulator for Community Interest Companies, and / or Companies House (don't worry – we'll touch upon these in Ch 4).

Firstly then, 'paperwork' and record-keeping: this includes scheduling meetings, taking notes in meetings and preparing and circulating the 'minutes'[3/4] etc. This is because the committee needs an accurate record of what was spoken about, by whom, and what was decided, what tasks were allocated, to whom, etc. Otherwise at every meeting there will be misunderstandings and confusion as to what was said and agreed, which will lead to arguments or to simmering and alienating resentment, and very little would be achieved. It is also because there should be a record of everything that your committee discusses and agrees or dismisses.

The second half of the Secretary's role includes the need to: 'be familiar with the charity's governing document [later in this chapter], the legal responsibilities of charities under the Charities Act 2009…; help to ensure that charity trustees…. file annual reports etc; [and] ensure that their fellow Committee members are aware of the requirements to comply with the relevant codes such as the charity's Code of Conduct for Charity Trustees and the Charities Governance Code'.[5]

The role of Secretary is more about character traits than a specific skill-base though: your committee's Secretary will need to be detail-oriented, meticulous and hard-working.

Treasurer – Perhaps surprisingly, for Treasurers too it's more about their character traits than their skills set: they will need integrity, and to be honest, detail-oriented, meticulous and hard-working.

Fundamentally, this role involves effectively monitoring and recording the Project's income and expenditure, and communicating that accurately to the committee. Done properly, and with meticulous attention to detail, this will also ensure that the Project's assets are protected, and the risk of theft or fraud, poor decision-making or mistakes is significantly reduced. But your Treasurer won't be doing this alone – ultimately *everyone* on the committee has a duty to protect the group's resources in order to fulfil your Project's aims. An essential read for everyone on the committee is the UK Government's 'Internal Financial Controls for Charities'[6], not least because everyone will need to be part of the decisions as to what financial procedures and controls are appropriate, and to make sure they are adhered to. The document just mentioned covers everything from the role of internal controls and reporting structures, to paying expenses and the acceptable process for handling cash donations. And, on that, your group will need a bank account before you start receiving donated money, and that brings up a key feature of internal financial controls – ensuring that no one person has 'sole responsibility for any single transaction from authorisation to completion and review'[7]. So you'll need to decide which committee members can be a cheque signatory (name three people – usually the Chair, the Treasurer and one other – and any two of these should be needed to sign any cheque). You and your Treasurer will also want to read a Government document called 'Charities and Risk Management'[6], and share that learning with the committee.

Other key roles

The first three roles detailed here concern the overall management, administration and finances of your Project. You will also need five additional committee members to take the lead in five different aspects of the Project: Safeguarding, Health and Safety, Data Protection, Communications, and Volunteer Management. We'll talk more about what is involved in those roles in the chapter covering Policies (chapter 9). (And for Volunteer Management, in chapter 10 too). This is because it is much easier to understand these five additional lead roles alongside the policies that the post-holders would need to implement.

Your group's 'rule book' – your committee is going to need to agree on a set of rules, or a 'Governing document'. This sets out the group's purposes or 'objects' (see chapter 4), and the framework for how your committee will be run. Everyone involved in the group will need to follow these rules, including all committee members, other key volunteers who help with the management of the charity, and any paid staff. There is guidance too on the website of The Association of Chairs[8].

Naming your Project – the name of your Project will probably reflect the help that you'll be providing – e.g. the 'Pumpernickel Street school uniform swap', or the 'Faux Area Gateaux and Gossip group for older people'. Even with these open access groups though, you may need to be discreet about what your group does, to protect the dignity of your service users. So, for example, perhaps a free meals service for young families could be called 'Dining as a Family at the – Centre' or something equally innocuous.

At this stage it would be useful to appeal for a couple of volunteers from within the committee to set up a fundraising sub-committee, to carry out some initial research into what funding opportunities might be available to the Project, and the turn-around for each potential funder's decision-making.

Further reading: Charity Excellence Framework (9) (free to register and use) is an organisation that provides very useful guidance to UK

Charities on a wide range of topics, from being a good trustee and a more effective Board, to securing funding and identifying sources of free resources. They'll come up again in chapter 9 (on Policies and Insurance) and chapter 7 (Fundraising).

JO'S STORY

Mid-March: Jo, the Chair of the committee, discussed her research findings with her fellow committee members, and asked for comments and suggestions. Ranya pointed out that a great many families would struggle to afford the gas or electricity required to reheat the food given as takeaway meals. Anne pointed out that it was isolating enough having a young family, but that having too little money coming in made this isolation more acute. She suggested that the meals be eaten communally, making it more of an occasion and enabling the families to socialise. Stuart said that this would also give the team the opportunity to let the families know about any other initiatives available locally that they might benefit from. And Magda highlighted that the packaging involved in providing takeaway meals would be damaging to the environment.

It was decided unanimously to provide a free communal meals service rather than a takeaway service, and to name the initiative the 'Family Dining Project'.

Jo said that when they knew approximately how many families could benefit from the Project, how often the service would run, and what they would need in terms of equipment and venue hire costs, they would begin to submit funding applications. She asked for volunteers from the committee to form a fundraising sub-committee, to begin some initial research into potential sources of funding for the Project. Anne and Sanjay offered to take this on and, as they were both conscientious and methodical, their help was gratefully accepted. They registered free with Charity Excellence Framework, and subsequently researched and considered all the potential sources of funding referenced on their website, noting that decisions from funders could take around three or four months.

ENDNOTES

1. Margaret Mead

2. The Complete Idiot's Guide to Recruiting and Managing Volunteers. John L. Lipp (2009) pub. By Alpha – a member of Penguin Group (USA) Inc.

3. From the Small Charities Coalition. 'Minutes need to include: The date of the meeting, who was present, what decisions were made. Decisions include: That the minutes of the previous meeting were approved as a correct record, approval of a document or accounts, [and] agreements made about spending money.' This organisation closed in 2022, and according to a message on their website: 'The FSI (the Foundation for Social Improvement) and NCVO (National Council for Voluntary Organisations) have come together to provide a home for the SCC Helpdesk and other key services'. https://www.thefsi.org/

4. https://www.charitiesregulator.ie/media/1688/guidance-note-on-minute-taking.pdf – 'This document is issued by the Charities Regulator under section 14(1)(i) of the Charities Act 2009, to encourage and facilitate the better administration and management of charitable organisations.'

5. https://www.charitiesregulator.ie/media/1722/the-role-of-the-secretary-of-a-charity.pdf – 'This document is issued by the Charities Regulator under section 14(1)(i) of the Charities Act 2009, to encourage and facilitate the better administration and management of charitable organisations.'

6. https://www.gov.uk/government/publications/internal-financial-controls-for-charities-cc8 – within which is an NCVO publication called 'The Honorary Treasurer's Handbook' which is referenced.

7. Charities and Risk Management (CC26) www.gov.uk/government/publications/charities-and-risk-management-cc26

8. Association of Chairs website (referred to by NCVO) https://www.associationofchairs.org.uk/

9. charityexcellence.co.uk

4

CHOOSING A STRUCTURE
FOR YOUR PROJECT

At first glance, this chapter may look a little dauntingly jam-packed with information. But you'll quickly see that it's just a chance to learn more about all of the main options open to you, and to weigh each against the others. It is a big decision. You'll soon identify the options that attract you most, and those that you would dismiss. Then it just becomes some essential information about the one or two that you would consider, and – when you have decided – the next steps in terms of the relevant organisation to guide your application. You might be thinking that this chapter doesn't apply to you – after all, you and your committee are prepared to keep going on your current relatively informal footing. However, there are disadvantages in not adopting a particular status for your group: the entire committee could be personally liable for any debts incurred through your Project-related activities; your access to funding is likely to be severely restricted if you have no legal structure in place; and you won't be perceived by external groups and organisations as being there 'for the long haul', with all that implies in terms of their investment of time and resources for your Project.

Any not-for-profit group carrying out exclusively charitable activities for the public benefit can apply to the Charity Commission for charitable status, and in this chapter I'll outline the three main options to choose from, and the reasons why you might decide to choose one option over the others. I'll also be looking at 'Community Interest Companies' (CICs), which allow more commercial flexibility, while a reasonable share of your Project's profits would benefit the community, either directly or indirectly. I've included (ordinary) Companies Limited by Guarantee here too, because groups do occasionally choose this option and, if you would be among those, in-depth accurate information on it is not easy to find.

There are four *main* options to choose from when deciding how your group is going to be set up: a Charitable Unincorporated Association, a Charitable Company (limited by guarantee), a Charitable Incorporated Organisation (CIO) and a Community Interest Company (CIC). And among the other rather more niche options there are (ordinary) Companies Limited by Guarantee, as I've mentioned. Of these five then, four give your committee members some (but not total) protection from personal liability for any debts incurred by the Project's activities, and one (i.e. a Charitable Unincorporated Association) does not. That said, even for Charitable Unincorporated Associations, it is very rare for trustees to be prosecuted if they've been 'acting in good faith' – i.e. demonstrably playing fair – but that doesn't mean *never*; and 'trustees' here means everyone on your committee (i.e. everyone involved in governance within your group), not necessarily just the people with the title of 'trustee'[1].

I'll begin with a 'wish list', so you can think about which features of each option would be important to your group.

- **Doesn't need an income to set up** – i.e. a Charitable Unincorporated Association, a Charitable Incorporated Organisation (CIO), a Community Interest Company (CIC) and a Company Limited by Guarantee.

- **Covers the committee from personal liability for any debts incurred by the group** – i.e. a Charitable Company (limited by guarantee), a Charitable

Incorporated Organisation (CIO), a Community Interest Company (CIC) and a Company Limited by Guarantee.

- **Enables your group to enter into contracts in the group's name** – i.e. a Charitable Company (limited by guarantee), a Charitable Incorporated Organisation (CIO), a Community Interest Company (CIC) and a Company Limited by Guarantee.

- **Enables your group to employ staff and own property in the group's name** – i.e. a Charitable Company (limited by guarantee), a Charitable Incorporated Organisation (CIO), a Community Interest Company (CIC) and a Company Limited by Guarantee.

- **Has minimal paperwork / hoops to jump through** – relatively speaking, a Charitable Unincorporated Association, a Charitable Incorporated Organisation (CIO) or a Company Limited by Guarantee.

- **Allows the option to fundraise** – technically this is all of them, but it is more limited for Community Interest Companies (CICs) and even more so for Companies Limited by Guarantee.

- **Benefits from tax relief** – 'Tax exemptions include income or corporation tax, stamp duty, land tax, inheritance tax on gifts made in wills and some VAT... And large reductions, if not complete exemptions, from paying business rates.'[2] – a Charitable Unincorporated Association, a Charitable Company (limited by guarantee), a Charitable Incorporated Organisation (CIO).

A CHARITABLE UNINCORPORATED ASSOCIATION

It's difficult to find a good reason for choosing this one over any of the other charity options detailed here, so I'm really just getting it out of the way first. A Charitable Unincorporated Association does not have a legal identity in its own right. So:

- Each committee member is personally liable for any debts or other liabilities incurred through the organisation's operations. For example, if rent or utility costs for a venue were incurred by the Project's activities, and there wasn't sufficient money in the pot, then the committee members would need to pay that out of their own pockets.

- Your group won't be able to enter into contracts in its own name, or borrow money. Instead, that responsibility must be assumed by one or more individuals within the group who are then held *personally* liable (although they would be well advised to enter into a separate agreement with the other committee members under which everyone agrees to contribute towards the cost). So, for example, if your group needed to hire cooking equipment in order to provide a service, or have a rental agreement for a van, that hire agreement would need to be in one person's name.

- Your group would have to follow Charity Commission rules and guidance, complying with charity law and subject to the Charity Commission's regulatory powers in the same way as incorporated charities.

- Regarding financial reporting[2], if your income is less than £10,000, you only need to report your income and spending to the Charity Commission annually. If it's between £10,000 and £25,000, you would need to answer questions about your charity in an annual return.

The questions you will be asked depend on your charity's income, the type of charity and what the charity does. You won't need to include any other documents. For income over £25,000 (and under £1,000,000), you'll also need to provide copies of your Trustee Annual Report, and accounts, and a report on your accounts by an independent examiner.

- The group is unable to own property or land, so two or more 'holding' trustees must hold that in their name (and ideally the holding trustees should be separate people from the charity trustees), or a corporate custodian trustee could be appointed to hold it. A custodian trustee would be a corporate body like a Parish Council or the Official Custodian of Charities. This body would hold the title on behalf of the charity, but wouldn't take any part in the charity's day-to-day operations or management.

- The group cannot employ staff in its own name. So an individual or individuals must assume the responsibilities of an employer.

However, as an organisation with Charity status, a Charitable Unincorporated Association would (in the same way as a CIO or Charitable Company limited by guarantee):

- Benefit from tax relief and could claim Gift Aid

- Be exempt from corporation tax

- Have the option to apply to those many Trusts and Foundations that only consider funding organisations with charitable status

- Benefit from the public trust and confidence that come from charitable status, because of all the regulatory checks and because your Project will be perceived as basically well-meaning and altruistic. This encourages people to donate their money (and time). And there are certain tax benefits for donors when giving money to a charity.

So, as with all groups with charity status, a Charitable Unincorporated Association could benefit from tax relief, and has access to a wide pool of potential funders. At the same time, like a CIO or Charitable Company Limited by Guarantee, Charitable Unincorporated Associations are required to adhere to charity law, and to submit financial information to the Charity Commission annually. Crucially, though, Unincorporated Associations lack the personal financial protection that is provided by an incorporated group.

If your group decides that it wants to remain unincorporated, NCVO recommends considering buying Trustee Indemnity Insurance and may recommend an insurer to you too[3].

CHARITABLE COMPANY (LIMITED BY GUARANTEE)

The first point I should make here is that your group would need to demonstrate an initial income** of at least £5000 to become a Charitable Company – and that if your group does have this income, and is carrying out exclusively charitable activities, you MUST register it with the Charity Commission. Charitable Companies (limited by Guarantee) have a corporate body, which means having a legal identity in their own right, like a person, enabling them to:

- Employ paid staff in the Project's name

- Enter into commercial contracts in the Project's name

- Own freehold or leasehold land or other property in the Project's name

AND

- Trustees 'acting in good faith' are very unlikely to be personally liable for the debts incurred by the group's activities.

PLUS

- Charitable Companies have charitable status, so again your group would benefit from tax relief and could claim Gift Aid

- And you'll be exempt from corporation tax

- And again you will have the option to apply to those many Trusts and Foundations that only consider those with charitable status

- And again, your group will benefit from the public trust and confidence that comes from charitable status, because of all the regulatory checks and because your Project will be perceived as basically well-meaning and altruistic. This encourages people to donate their money (and time). And there are certain tax benefits for donors when giving money to a charity

- Becoming a Charitable Company will mean that you are taken seriously by other organisations in the Third Sector; you've demonstrably jumped through all the hoops, and you'll be perceived as intending to operate for the long term.

HOWEVER

- Your group needs an initial income of at least £5000 per year to set this up. (In exceptional circumstances you may be permitted to register with the Charity Commission without this income – if, for example, you could prove that you've had an offer of substantial funding based on having a registered charity number. But it wouldn't be enough to argue that you could apply for funding if you had this – anyone could do that!)

- As with other types of charity, your group would have to be registered with and report to the Charity Commission, and follow Charity Commission rules and guidance, complying with charity law and subject to the Charity Commission's regulatory powers

- And additionally you will be required to register with Companies House, and adhere to the Companies Act 2006

- And produce a Trustees' annual report – giving an account of the charity's performance

- According to the Charity Commission website, Charitable Companies' financial reports to the Charity Commission are the same as for unincorporated organisations: if your income is less than £10,000, you only need to report your income and spending to them annually. If it's between £10,000 and £25,000, you would need to answer questions about your charity in an annual return. The questions you will be asked depend on your income, the type of charity and what the charity does. You won't need to include any other documents. For income over £25,000 (and under £1,000,000), you'll also need a report of your accounts by an independent examiner, and to provide copies of your trustee annual report, and accounts.

So, you need an income of at least £5000 per year to set this up. You have the advantages of charitable status for fundraising and tax relief, with the financial reporting tasks of a Charitable Unincorporated Association, and you must adhere to charity law. Plus you would need to adhere to the regulations of the Companies Act 2006. You would have the personal financial protection provided by being an incorporated group.

CHARITABLE INCORPORATED ORGANISATION (CIO)

CIOs were introduced in 2013, and are now the most common form for incorporated not-for-profit groups in the UK. Like Charitable Companies, a CIO has a 'corporate body' and so has a legal identity in its own right. So if your group decided to become a CIO, it would have the legal capacity to do many things in its own name that a person can do, such as:

- Employing paid staff

- Entering into commercial contracts

- Owning freehold or leasehold land or other property.

AND

- Trustees acting in good faith are very unlikely to be personally liable for the debts incurred by the group's activities

- Your group doesn't need any income to set this up.

PLUS

- CIOs have charitable status, like Charitable Unincorporated Associations and Charitable Companies limited by guarantee, so again your group would benefit from tax relief and could claim Gift Aid

- You'll be exempt from Corporation Tax

- And again you will have the option to apply to many Trusts and Foundations that only consider those with charitable status

- There are comparatively simpler reporting requirements when compared to Charitable Companies, as CIOs don't need to register with Companies House

- Charitable status also promotes public trust and confidence, because of all the regulatory checks, and because your Project will be perceived as basically well-meaning and altruistic. This encourages people to donate their money and time. And there are certain tax benefits for donors when giving money to a charity

- Becoming a CIO will – like a Charitable Company – mean that you are taken seriously by other organisations in the Third Sector; you've demonstrably jumped through all the hoops, and you'll be perceived as intending to operate for the long term.

HOWEVER

- As with other types of charity, your group would have to be registered with and report to the Charity Commission, and follow Charity Commission rules and guidance, complying with charity law and subject to the Charity Commission's regulatory powers

- Your group would have to produce a trustees' annual report, giving an account of the charity's performance

- Regarding financial reporting[2], if your income is under £25,000 you must answer questions about your charity in an annual return to the Charity Commission, and include copies of your trustee annual report and accounts. And if your income is over £25,000 (and under £1,000,000) you would also need to get your accounts checked and submit a copy of the independent examiner's report.

So, you do not need any income to set a CIO up. You have the advantages of charitable status for fundraising and tax relief, with the financial reporting tasks and other regulations imposed by the Charity Commission, and you must adhere to charity law.

But you would not be affected by the Companies Act 2006. You have the personal financial protection provided by being an incorporated group.

Unregistered charities

Charities which are not obliged to register with the Charity Commission (i.e. those charities with an annual income under £5000, who don't want to become CIOs) can at least apply to HMRC for the tax reliefs available to charities, and use their HMRC charity number as evidence of charitable status. 'They must still comply with charity law, but this does not include filing annual returns [with the Charity Commission], so there will not be the same administrative responsibility as a registered charity; it simply must be a lawful charitable entity.'[2] Unregistered charities must just report income and spending to the Charity Commission, annually.

Just a word here on 'Charitable Objects'

Before we move from groups with charitable status, I'll just mention charitable 'objects'. A charity's 'objects' are a statement of its charitable purposes – i.e. what the charity has been set up to achieve and how it is of benefit to the public. There are thirteen charitable objects to choose from[2] within the Charity Commission's list, including: the relief of poverty; advancing education; health; and environmental protection or improvement. Basically your charitable objects will spell out what your group does, who it helps, where it operates and how it works. Your Charitable Objects will feature in your application to the Charity Commission, and will underpin the decisions that yourself and your fellow trustees make and how the charity is run. There is guidance on writing your charity's objects on the Charity Commission's website[2] –if you're unsure about anything, just ask them. They will want to help you.

COMMUNITY INTEREST COMPANY (CIC)

If you'd prefer to run your group with more commercial flexibility but with social, environmental or community-based benefits, you could set up a Community Interest Company (CIC) – pronounced 'kick'. This benefit could be directly delivered by the CIC to a specific community – for example, some foodbanks are CICs – or some of the profits could be used to benefit a specific community. The National Council for Voluntary Organisations (NCVO) has provided examples of CICs, and some avenues for guidance on setting them up[4].

CICs are incorporated companies, so, in the group's name, you could:

- Hire staff

- Enter into contracts

- Own assets

- Have the option of borrowing money

- And the option to fund-raise.

AND

- There are fewer reporting requirements and less administration than for those with charity status: your group would **not** need to follow Charity Commission rules and guidance, comply with charity law or be subject to the Charity Commission's regulatory powers. According to the website of the CIC Regulator[5], there has been an increase in conversions to CICs from registered charities, and there is a suggestion from the Regulator that this is because the regulations involved in charity status are time-consuming and rather burdensome

- Your group would have a greater flexibility in terms of activities that you can carry out, as you don't need to work strictly within the parameters of 'charitable purposes'

- CICs offer some reassurance to potential funders, as the company's 'community purpose' is regulated through an annual 'Community Interest Report' to the Government's Office of the Regulator of Community Interest Companies, and the company's assets are 'locked' (more about these two in the 'However' section!)

- The application to the CIC Regulator to form a Community Interest Company, if approved, allows a CIC to register their company name with Companies House and register with HMRC for Corporation Tax, all at the same time.

HOWEVER

- Access to funding will be more limited than for those with charity status. CICs may be greeted with some suspicion by both the public and community groups, particularly as most people do not know about the restrictions imposed on the assets of CICs, or indeed anything else about CICs. That said, to some extent availability of funding sources may depend on which geographical area your company will cover, and the activities that you're going to be carrying out – i.e. if it needs doing and no-one else is doing it in that area, you're more likely to attract funding

- Like any business, you would need to register with Companies House and adhere to the Companies Act 2006

- And, like any business, you'd need to make a profit to survive

- Financial reporting – your group would need to submit annual company accounts and returns to Companies House

- And you must also complete a 'Community Interest Report' annually, for the CIC Regulator. This must demonstrate that your company has devoted a 'reasonable' proportion of your profits to benefit the community you serve. The Regulator doesn't stipulate the percentage of profits that must benefit the community. Instead this is what a *reasonable* person would consider fair. The Community Interest Report needs to set out exactly how the CIC has met its obligations to deliver community benefits. It will also contain additional financial information such as payments to directors, and the use of assets

- No tax breaks

- Cannot claim Gift Aid on donations

- Must register for Corporation Tax within three months of starting to trade[6], as all non-charitable companies are liable to Corporation Tax on their profits, subject to any specific exemptions (which you'd need to speak with an accountant about)

- The 'asset lock' ensures that assets are kept within the company to support its activities or otherwise used to benefit the community. If a CIC is dissolved, any surplus assets must be transferred to another asset-locked body, once all liabilities have been met

- Once you've set up a CIC, you cannot in the future change this to a 'normal' Limited Company. If you no longer want to run your company as a CIC the only options would be either to change to registered charity status, or to dissolve the company.

N.B. CICs need Directors and Members***. However, while they serve two separate functions, they are not necessarily two different sets of people: the directors could be the only members.

COMPANY LIMITED BY GUARANTEE (CLG)

A Company Limited by Guarantee (CLG) is essentially a not-for-profit organisation: there are no shareholders and no dividends, and therefore the profits are ploughed back into furthering the aims of the company. The likelihood is that these aims will be for the public benefit, but that they may fall outside the thirteen 'charitable purposes' stipulated by the Charity Commission. That might just make you a trailblazer though – at one time the 'advancement of environmental protection or improvement' wasn't a 'charitable purpose'. There is some useful guidance on setting up these companies at NVCO[7] and Companies House[8]. CLGs (like CICs) need Directors and Members***. However, while they serve two separate functions, they are not necessarily two different sets of people: in a lot of CLGs (and CICs), the directors are the only members.

Having a legal entity in its own right, a CLG is able to:

- employ paid staff in its own name

- enter into commercial contracts in its own name

- own freehold or leasehold land or other property in its own name.

AND

- The liability of its *Directors* is limited as CLGs are incorporated, though Directors can still be liable in certain circumstances – such as fraudulent activity. Each *Member's* liability is limited to the amount of the guarantee stipulated in the company's Articles of Association – which is typically just £1.00 (it's up to you when drafting the Articles of Association what limit to stipulate****)

- Your group doesn't need any income to be allowed to set up a CLG

- As with a CIC, your group would have a greater flexibility in terms of activities that you can carry out, compared to a charitable organisation, as you won't need to work strictly within the parameters of 'charitable purposes'

- A CLG, like a CIC, does not report to the Charity Commission, and so is not required to follow Charity Commission rules and guidance.

PLUS

- Loans are a possibility – though, as banks and other lenders will often ask for their money to be secured against certain assets of the company, the possibility of obtaining a loan will often be dependent on the extent and nature of the assets of the CLG, as is the case with any other type of company

- Members sometimes fund a CLG through paying a membership fee. This would typically only be the case if the members receive some benefit from that membership in return; this isn't financial – there are no shareholders or dividends paid – but rather involvement, 'having a say' in an organisation that means something to them. If the organisation provides a service, it could be that members get preferential treatment too

- Unlike for CICs, there is no Community Interest Report to complete and submit annually

- And the assets of a CLG are not locked as those of a CIC are – though that would make funders more cautious.

HOWEVER

- Like a CIC, your group won't have charitable status

- While grant funding *may* be available to an ordinary CLG if it meets the relevant grant funder's criteria, a CLG is less attractive to funders than charitable status and – to a lesser extent – CIC status

- Whilst it is very unlikely for Directors to be personally liable if they act sensibly and within the law, in the very rare cases in which Directors can be personally liable, that liability could in principle be limitless

- Must register at Companies House (as with Charitable Companies Limited by Guarantee and CICs)

- Financial reporting – your group would need to submit annual company accounts and returns to Companies House

- Must register for Corporation Tax within three months of starting to trade, as all non-charitable companies (including CICs) are liable to pay Corporation Tax on their profits, subject to any specific exemptions. (Only charitable status automatically exempts you from Corporation Tax)

- And, like any business, you'd need to make a profit to survive

- There are no automatic tax breaks

- CLGs cannot claim Gift Aid on donations

- There are reputational disadvantages for ordinary CLG status when compared to CIC status: the latter is registered as doing something in the community interest, which can impress third parties. And CICs can more convincingly style themselves as 'social enterprises' than can ordinary CLGs, and there is some support targeted at helping social enterprises

- Networking – while CICs are now routinely included in network meetings in the Third Sector, I believe that this could be more difficult for most CLGs.

If you wanted to start your Project and run it for a time to make sure that it was well-received and well-supported before applying for charitable status (if your aims fall within one of the thirteen charitable purposes), you could begin as an ordinary Company Limited by Guarantee, knowing that the process to change to a Charitable Company later on is not too difficult. The Charity Commission has published a set of model articles suitable for companies limited by guarantee that intend to register as charities[10]. If you begin as a CIC though, it is rather more onerous to convert to charitable status.

So, a CLG is a type of company, and this in itself provides Directors with some protection from personal liability. However, Directors can still be liable in certain circumstances, and in principle that liability could be limitless. CLGs must also register with Companies House and adhere to the Companies Act (2006), like Charitable Companies and CICs. As with CICs, CLGs must register for Corporation Tax. Again like CICs, there are no automatic tax exemptions, and CLGs cannot claim Gift Aid. Fundraising opportunities are even more limited than for CICs. However, all that said, it requires less admin than CICs - as there is no Community Interest Report to complete annually. And the assets of a CLG are not 'locked' as they are with CICs. And it is more straightforward for CLGs to change to having charitable status than it is for CICs, though you don't have the reputational or networking benefits of being registered as a social enterprise.

Table summarising the main points of the five types of group status outlined in this chapter

	Charitable Unincorporated Association	Charitable Company (limited by guarantee)	Charitable Incorporated Organisation (CIO)	Community Interest Company (CIC)	Company Limited by Guarantee (CLG)
No initial income needed	YES		YES	YES	YES
Personal liability protection		YES	YES	YES	YES
Enter into contracts in the Project's name		YES	YES	YES	YES
Employ staff in the Project's name		YES	YES	YES	YES
Access to a wide range of grants from potential funders	YES	YES	YES		

Tax relief / Gift Aid	YES	YES	YES		
Register with Companies House		YES		YES	YES
Follow Charity Commission rules and guidance	YES	YES	YES		
Register for Corporation Tax				YES	YES
Enjoy public trust from the outset	YES	YES	YES		
Less strict parameters for operating				YES	YES

Why my preference would be for becoming a Charitable Incorporated Organisation (CIO) or a Community Interest Company (CIC)

Firstly, I am risk averse, and I expect that you are too: being 'unincorporated' – i.e. being a Charitable Unincorporated Association – means that you and everyone involved in managing your Project will be personally liable for debts incurred while your group is operating if the organisation runs out of money (or in some circumstances – for example, involving fraud – even if it does not). Additionally, unincorporated charities have all the administrative tasks and regulatory controls of groups with charity status, and must still follow Charity Commission rules and guidance, complying with charity law and subject to the Charity Commission's regulatory powers. The Charity Commission can investigate even small unincorporated charities.

Setting up a Charitable Company requires that your group has the necessary initial £5000 minimum income. Even with that though, many groups that originally chose to become a Charitable Company are themselves changing to a CIO, because of the extra administrative burden on Charitable Companies – namely, having to register with Companies House and adhere to the Companies Act (2006) in addition to the other expectations of those with charity status.

For groups wanting charity registration, that leaves CIOs – the most administratively straightforward of the incorporated options, and currently the most popular among those wanting charity status.

For groups that want the protections of being incorporated, but who would prefer to run a Project in a commercially more flexible way but which will also benefit the community, then choosing to become a CIC might be the right choice, if you can manage without the greater access to funding and the tax benefits of charity status. While Companies Limited by Guarantee do not need to complete an annual Community Interest Report and do not have their assets 'locked' as CICs do, they have even more limited access to grant funding, and they do not have the reputational or networking benefits of being registered as a social enterprise.

While you're making your choice, and when you've decided, there is a great deal of information and support to be found from both the National Council for Voluntary Organisations (NCVO) and the Foundation for Social Improvement***** (FSI)[11]. NCVO will also know of free and low-cost legal advice that you could access.

Next steps

Charitable Unincorporated Associations, Charitable Companies (limited by guarantee) and Charitable Incorporated Organisations (CIOs) all have 'charitable status'. If you'd like your group to become a Charitable Unincorporated Association, Charitable Company or a CIO, you'll need to visit the UK Government's Charity Commission website for detailed guidance etc. CICs do not have charitable status, and to apply to set one up you'll need to visit the website of the UK Government's Office of the Regulator for Community Interest Companies. To register as a Company Limited by Guarantee, you would need to apply to Companies House[12].

Further Reading

NCVO recommends a guide[13] which explains some of the different legal structures and their associated advantages and disadvantages. This covers Unincorporated Associations, CIOs, Companies Limited by Guarantee and CICs (and includes some more niche choices), and has some case studies too which might be of interest.

JO'S STORY

Mid-March: The Family Dining Committee discussed the possible options to choose from for the status of their Project that Jo had researched. No-one wanted to risk having to use their own money to pay off debts incurred by the Project, and so dismissed the option of being a Charitable Unincorporated

Association. The Project didn't have the necessary initial £5000 minimum income to set up a Charitable Company, but they didn't want the extra administrative burden of complying with the Companies Act (2006) anyway. The Committee did want charity registration though – because of the fundraising and reputational advantages, and the tax breaks – and everyone was attracted to the very popular Charitable Incorporated Organisation (CIO) model, because it was the most administratively straightforward of the incorporated options. They completed and submitted their application.

Jo and the committee had considered Community Interest Companies and Companies Limited by Guarantee, just in case they offered advantages over a charity model. But it was felt that neither of these would be a good fit for them, as their service users would not be paying any money for the meals, so the Project would have no income to make up for the reduced access to external funding available to CICs and CLGs.

ENDNOTES

---

* Your charity structure is defined by its 'governing document' (a legal document that creates the charity and details how it should be run – a rulebook really). There are model documents on the Charity Commission website. Templates for the documents needed for CICs are to be found on the website of the Government's Office of the Regulator for Community Interest Companies – and for Companies Limited by Guarantee, from Companies House.

** In theory the test is an annual income of £5,000 per year, but in practice the Charity Commission will settle for proof that a Charitable Company Limited by Guarantee has a starting income of £5,000 (or a promise of funding of £5,000 from a recognised funding body). This makes sense, because at the time of applying for registration you often cannot realistically prove that you will definitely have an income over £5,000 in future years. And there are certainly charities on the register whose annual income is well below that (and which are not CIOs).

*** If you give someone full membership it confers a lot of power on them – including the ability to vote to change the constitution or to remove Directors. However if you wanted a membership in addition to your Directors you could instead have 'Associate Members', e.g. 'Friends of...'

**** Model Articles of Association for Companies Limited by Guarantee have been established by legislation – i.e. the Companies (Model Articles) Regulations 2008(9), which may be used with or without amendment, or alternatively bespoke articles of association may be used. (Whether you use the model articles or bespoke articles, you might need a solicitor to help with this process, at the very least so as to understand what you are committing to).

***** FSI replaced the Small Charities Coalition.

1. From the Charity Commission's website – The National Council for Voluntary Organisations (NCVO) has produced the following guidance: https://blogs.ncvo. org.uk/wp-content/uploads/guest/trustee-liability-guide. pdf - Trustee liability guide. Summary of the potential personal liabilities associated with becoming the trustee of a charity.

2. The Charity Commission's website – https://www.gov.uk/ government/organisations/charity-commission

3. https://knowhow.ncvo.org.uk/organisation/operations/ insurance

4. https://beta.ncvo.org.uk/help-and-guidance/setting-up/ understanding-social-enterprise/

5. https://www.gov.uk/government/organisations/office-of-the-regulator-of-community-interest-com panies

6. From 'Community Companies: A Company Law Solutions Company' website https://www. communitycompanies.co.uk/companies-limited-by-guarantee#intro

7. via NCVO – https://www.gov.uk/set-up-limited-company

8. via Companies House – https://www.gov.uk/limited-company-formation

9. https://www.gov.uk/guidance/model-articles-of-association-for-limited-companies

10. https://www.gov.uk/government/publications/setting-up-
    a-charity-model-governing-documents

11. https://www.thefsi.org.

12. https://www.gov.uk/limited-company-formation/ register-
    your-company

13. Produced by The Thomson Reuters Foundation
    partnered with Morrison & Foerster and UnLtd.

    https://www.trust.org/contentAsset/raw-data/fb362caf-
    6795-4f23-aa20-212b9654e877/file

5

COMMUNICATIONS WITH LOCAL GROUPS AND ORGANISATIONS, AND RECORD-KEEPING

This chapter covers: who you will need to speak with; what you would communicate, i.e. what information you would provide, and when, and what you should (and should not) ask for; follow-up tips and timescales; and maintaining good communication. We'll also cover record-keeping here, as this is absolutely crucial to prevent you losing track of your progress.

There are different stages to your communications, from your initial awareness-raising and subsequent request for guidance and information, to keeping everyone updated as to progress, and generating referrals to your service when it's up and running. We'll cover all of these. It's essential to have the right tone in all your communications. Communicating with external groups is about the same as speaking with colleagues at work when there's a customer or client present: neither too formal nor too informal – politely neutral. But communication is always a two-way street, and you'll need to spend a considerable amount of time listening to local groups and organisations too. This will give you invaluable information, provide access to potentially useful networks and resources, and enable you to build mutually beneficial relationships. Crucially, you'll also need to evaluate what you are told, in the light of your research and knowledge, and recognise incorrect information when you hear it.

Be clear about what you want from every communication

Keep your goals to the forefront of your mind with every communication, to make sure that your Project – whatever that looks like – fulfils the promise of your lightbulb moment. To achieve this, you need to be clear about what you want from any communication.

> *For example, for my first presentation – in the time before PowerPoint presentations – I practised for days, and by the time I was standing in front of the group I barely needed to glance at my prompt cards. I delivered a well-rounded talk about the subject (if I do say so myself!), projecting my voice to the back of the room, and there were nods of agreement as I spoke. I triumphantly got to 'Any questions?' when someone asked 'But, what do you want?'*

Since then, I've been guided in every communication by Rudyard Kipling's 'Six honest serving men': 'I keep six honest serving-men (They taught me all I know); their names are What and Why and When and How and Where and Who.'

The two questions that should guide your communications

- Who do you need to speak with?
- What do you want from the communication?

Who do you need to speak with?

Your research will have identified the locally based groups and organisations that are providers of a service similar to your planned provision, and / or support the same service users that you are working to help. You'll be starting by contacting these. They will inevitably lead to others and they to others still. Dive in! It may take a little bit of phoning around and / or website-based research to identify the person that you will need to speak with in each organisation or group – it could be a Community Engagement Officer, Development Officer, or the Manager of a particular initiative related to your Project. Do speak with the Chairpersons of relevant volunteer-led groups too, as their insights and experience will be invaluable – beginning your initial communications with 'I am the Chair of…' But before you approach them, check how the group is perceived by well-known local organisations, and why. You don't want to align yourselves with any group that is seen as disreputable.

What do you want from the communication?

Locally-based groups and organisations will not do your work for you! They may be generous with their time and resources – if it is within their remit and capacity to do so, and especially if it 'ticks a box' for them in terms of promises made to funders or members – but don't ask for anything that is not relevant to them, or outside their scope of experience or expertise. It won't get you anywhere, and may damage how your Project is perceived as it implies a lack of research.

Ask yourself what you need to know from these groups and organisations, and how they *can* help you progress your Project. You'll certainly want to find out:

- The 'What' and 'Where' of services they are delivering / planning to deliver / no longer delivering (and why)

- What their current focus is

- What research they have carried out, and whether you could access it

- Details of other organisations and community groups that might be a source of information and support, including small grassroots groups which might be just quietly delivering a service without any digital bells and whistles.

You'll also want

- Introductions – these are quicker and more productive than cold calling. So, once you've spent the time building a relationship with an organisation, ask them if they could introduce you to others in the area / network. Any email that begins with 'Peter Jones from the local Council kindly gave me your contact details' will get more attention than cold-calling, and should get a response. Incidentally this also demonstrates that you're in touch with the appropriate people and therefore that you're approaching this in the right way. (And if it doesn't get a response, just revisit Peter)

- An invitation to a meeting of the local relevant network, which is made up of organisations working in the same field as your proposed Project. Just ask the groups that you're now in touch with about joining the network – any member will be able to introduce you to the network's facilitator. Your aim here is twofold: profile-raising, and identifying further organisations and groups that could potentially support you in achieving your Project's goals. (See chapter 6 for guidance on presentations and meetings).

In your initial communications you need to demonstrate

- What you are planning
- Who will benefit
- And how your Project will add value.

I don't mean that you should send reams of unsolicited information to people – it won't be read. Revisit the 150 words that you wrote for chapter 1, and answer the same questions in the light of new information. Keep your re-drafted outline to the original 150 words limit – this will underpin your initial emails.

If you've had a positive response, your follow-up communications may need to show:

- What steps you've taken so far

- Who you've spoken with

- That you're aware of the work that is currently being done in the area to support the service users, and the ways in which your Project differs

- How your Project will help them to deliver *their* targets – e.g. signposting their service users to an appropriate service.

The Practicalities of Communication: Phone, email, text, speak, repeat!

Before you pick up the phone, think about (and write down) a few lines that introduce your Project. There are two versions to prepare: one for the person who would usually answer the phone initially within an organisation – a member of Reception staff or Admin – and a second slightly fuller outline in case you get the opportunity to speak with the person that you're trying to reach. Your first version might be along the lines of: 'Hi. This is [full name]. I'm the Chair of the Committee working to set up more [Nursery provision] in [area]. I'd like to speak with your [Early Years Officer] please.' If they are unavailable, then make sure that you find out their name, and of course their contact details. Ask for the name of the person who you are speaking with – this focuses people on making sure that they carry out your request. Ask that a message reaches [the Early Years Officer] that you phoned and why, and that you will be sending an email to them within the next few minutes (you'll already have drafted it, so it'll just need to be personalised). You could also ask for the email address of the person that you are speaking with – it may be the organisation's general email address – and then copy them in. This is just in case your email to the [Early Years Officer] goes into SPAM.

If the relevant person *is* available to speak with you, then you'll need a fuller introduction to your Project. This would also include, for example, 'I understand that [organisation] already supports [young families] to access provision / that this is a service that you have set up in other areas, and I'd like to arrange a time to speak with you if possible, to tell you more about our proposed service and to ask for your guidance and advice.' While it will be tempting to tell the person everything while you've got them on the phone, don't! A more in-depth explanation is probably going to involve too much information for anyone to take in 'cold', so, unless they have any initial questions, assure them that you'll send them an email summarising all the facts, and that you'll be in touch after they've had a chance to read it.

For either scenario, leave your contact details – and check that they've been taken down correctly. If you have a mobile phone number for the person you need to speak with, you should send a quick confirmatory text message just after sending the email, in case it goes into SPAM. Give them a week to get back to you.

Just a quick note here: if your research, and the knowledge gleaned from conversations with relevant Third Sector groups and organisations, leads you to believe that a particular organisation could be of help to you, don't allow yourself to be put off by the person who picks up the phone initially. Always be polite in your persistence, asking to speak with a member of the team that you need to access, bearing in mind that unfortunately some employers do not tell the gatekeepers for their organisations (e.g. staff on Reception or admin for a team) about ongoing or planned initiatives in good time.

The structure of your initial emails

- The email title and opening lines need to mention key words: A new Project supporting [a particular group of people] in [city / town] through [service provided]. You need to capture the interest of people very quickly indeed

- Tailor it to the organisation that you're contacting – sometimes you'll place more emphasis on one aspect of your service, and sometimes another. *For example, if your Project is a lunch club and you are contacting an organisation that supports lonely older people, you'd emphasise the social side. And if you were setting up a Community pantry, organisations supporting low income families would be interested in the low cost groceries*

- The main body of your email is your revised 150 words (i.e. who, what, how, why, when, where)

- No group emails. Each email must be addressed to the person you have identified as most relevant to your Project within each organisation. If you think about it, people reading your email will give it absolutely no attention if they see it as a 'circular', but will be obliged to at least read it if it is addressed to them personally. You'd probably be the same. And if you're perceived as someone who can't be bothered to send a tailored personalised email, will they think that you're going to be worth taking their time? You need to demonstrate that you've done your research

- Round off your emails with three actions:

  1. Reference the time frame for your Project – and hence the need to speak with them soon.

  2. Include a specific question that they need to respond to, e.g. 'Could we arrange to meet?' 'Would you like hard copies / how many / where to?' These can be difficult to resist answering.

  3. And finally thank them for their time. It's polite, and they may feel that they need to earn your thanks!

How and when do you follow up?

You've got a great idea that will help vulnerable people within the Community, and you can demonstrate the need. Follow up on your initial communications if you have had no response, by phone if at all possible. If you've had to contact people again to chase them, they are usually apologetic AND 'on the back foot', so more conducive to hearing you out. Be forgiving; it may have gone to their SPAM folder, or at least you can suggest that this might have happened. If you haven't heard back from someone though, and they're still proving elusive when you phone to speak with them after you've sent both the initial email and a polite nudge or two (i.e. a politely enquiring follow-up email, and a phone message), then after 2-3 weeks' waiting, you'll need to speak with their Line Manager. Anyone within the organisation should be able to tell you who that is. Yes, people are busy, and they won't have your sense of urgency with this. They may well have 'red-flagged' your email with the best intentions, where it joined all the other red-flagged emails. It might be that they're off sick or on holiday, and didn't put their 'out of office' message on, or they're covering two jobs. They could be lazy or overwhelmed. You never know. But after about 2-3 weeks you're going to need to take it up the chain.

Always be polite in your persistence – aside from absolutely everything else in terms of being a human being reacting to another person, you don't want to be dismissed as an annoyance, and you don't know what's going on for that person or within that organisation at the time. And your behaviour reflects on the Project that you're representing. That said, in the end you need something from that organisation – whether that's information, an introduction to a network meeting, etc – and you have to keep going until you get it, or at least until you understand the problem and an alternative staff member or option has been suggested to you. Don't be afraid to revisit organisations. People are busy but on the whole well-meaning, and they will generally help you if they are able to.

Keeping everyone in the loop

Keep everyone who has helped you or who continues to support your efforts or who represents relevant local groups and organisations – and these aren't mutually exclusive! – in the loop via email. This will entail very briefly highlighting key achievements and milestones every month or so, along with upcoming goals and challenges, and acknowledgements of all help and support. It's polite, and keeps the Project to the forefront of minds. And sometimes it will prompt someone to say 'Oh, if you're at that stage you'll want to speak with –. Here's their contact details.' Update your contacts regularly as to progress. When people have invested time and possibly resources into your Project, your successes are (vicariously) theirs too, which makes your challenges something they'll want to help you tackle, and offer suggestions to overcome. It's all part of good communication.

Record-keeping

You'll need a plan for this that works for you, before you dial your first phone number or send your first email. There are two main aspects to good Record-keeping: accuracy, and acting on your own prompts.

Accurate Record-keeping

You need to maintain an up-to-date detailed record of your progress, on paper or electronically (with back-ups), outlining:

- Who you've spoken with

- What the result of that communication was

- The next steps you've identified

- The gaps in your knowledge

- And who to approach to fill these gaps.

Take notes for every meeting or conversation you have related to your Project – the main points of what was said, who by, who they represent, dated, with a list of attendees if appropriate. Otherwise they will begin to blur into one – trust me! Keep a folder of emails from representatives of relevant organisations too, and a record of texts, or at least the main points they contain.

Your records will also be the basis of your regular report to your fellow committee members – and will give them an opportunity to contribute information on their own progress on behalf of the group. This report on progress and next steps will enable you, for example, to anticipate when you could usefully and productively schedule meetings with individuals representing local organisations, funders etc. (You'll need to give them adequate notice, and to be sufficiently prepared yourself – time is money in every sector!)

Acting on your own prompts

In part, record-keeping ensures that you keep on top of revisiting organisations and individuals who haven't replied to you: keep a diary of when you contacted people, and decide what day you'd reasonably expect to hear back from them, and on that date in your diary put a prompt to yourself to nudge them if you haven't heard. But it's also a prompt to remind you of meetings (naturally), and to respond to someone that you promised information to. Record it all in your diary – and act on these prompts.

A final word here

If at any time during this (admittedly somewhat lengthy) process, it's all feeling a bit too much, maybe arrange to visit a similar provision elsewhere, or a scheme helping the same service users in a different way – remind yourself what it's all for. It works every time!

6

WORKING WITH OTHER GROUPS AND ORGANISATIONS

Now it's time to reap the rewards of your work to date: the knowledge, contacts, networks and possibly the resources of these local groups and organisations could help you significantly in achieving your goal, and you'll be ensuring that you're not duplicating services. However, the work ahead with local groups and organisations does need to be demonstrably of benefit to them too. This is because – with the best will in the world – the Third Sector is stretched, and if you cannot demonstrate clearly and concisely that your Project will enable an organisation to further their service users' interests, or put a 'tick' next to something that they've promised their funders or members, they won't be able to devote much of their limited time and resources to you. You need organisations to realise that:

- Your Project will be both reputable and useful

- You will be helping them to achieve some of their targets through your Project, i.e. funders are likely to require them to build mutually supportive partnerships with groups delivering related services

- You will be signposting service users to *their* Projects – so increasing their client base.

This chapter will guide you through meetings with local groups and organisations, and delivering presentations. Don't worry, you'll make it look effortless – because 'Practice makes Professional'.

Some initial hints and tips

- Make a note of the correct pronunciations of peoples' names if you're unfamiliar with them. If you can't pronounce it, you're bound to have to introduce them to someone else – that *is* the way the world works!

- Remember what people tell you about themselves (write it down if you need to, as soon as you have a quiet moment) and show an interest when next you meet them. People are endlessly engrossing, and as a bonus they're much more likely to go the extra mile if they like you and see you as a genuine person, interested in them. This will help to create a connection

- Don't be too self-effacing. People you meet will usually take you on your own valuation of yourself. You represent your Project, so you're not brash but you are assured. You're confident rather than boastful. Your refreshing positivity and optimism is backed up by your knowledge and research

- A note on eye contact and posture: basically, maintaining eye contact is good, for a limited amount of time. Slouching can indicate indifference (and will remind everyone of stroppy teenagers). Crossing your arms is not good, because people often mistakenly interpret crossed arms as a way of keeping people away, or to indicate dislike[1]. I cross my arms when I'm tired, or to hide a coffee stain if

I've been even clumsier than usual. But as long as people hold these misconceptions, it's probably best to avoid doing it. But you can be somewhat reassured if you see it in others – it's probably just about a newly acquired coffee stain!

- Be a friendly face – people will seek you out.

The Etiquette of meetings

Everyone within meetings has something that they want to communicate – there's an etiquette to it that you need to be aware of, and your role is that of invited guest. Meetings will usually begin with an opportunity for each person to spend one minute giving their name, role and an outline of their organisation and current focus. Don't take longer than the time given: everyone is there to further the interests of the organisation that they represent and to identify others who can help them to achieve their organisation's goals.

Meetings

Since the first Covid lockdown there has been a huge shift from in-person meetings to virtual ones. Not having to travel makes meetings cheaper and saves time. A small disadvantage is not being able to chat more informally with potentially useful people in the coffee breaks, but that's easily overcome by contacting them (possibly via the facilitator until you have their contact details) after the virtual meeting.

For meetings, whether with representatives from a single organisation or several, make sure that you learn beforehand how your Project will advance each organisation's targets – do the work for them. And have a realistic idea of what support and / or resources might be available from them (for example, a reasonably priced or free venue* for your Project sessions, an introduction to a local network or to other relevant groups) and what won't be available (money or volunteers). At the time that you're invited to attend one of these meetings, ask the facilitator for a five minute time slot to give a brief presentation (we'll look at presentations later in this chapter).

Note down everyone as they introduce themselves and their respective organisations – marking down the ones that you might benefit from further contact with. If you're meeting virtually, you can easily request contact details directly from an attendee if the meeting platform has a 'chat' function. Send messages directly to any person who seems potentially useful straight away – and additionally send your contact details and one line summarising your proposed Project to 'Everyone' very early on. Don't wait until the end of the meeting; people may leave before the end of online meetings, especially if they overrun – not something that would usually happen in a face-to-face meeting.

Anticipate and prepare to answer questions from groups that might see your Project as a threat to their funding or attendees' numbers. Your research into unmet need will be invaluable here. Answer any questions calmly, and stay focused on the facts, e.g. that, as far as you're aware, the area that you're setting up in currently has no similar service running for that group of service users, or not on that day, or not without a referral... And if questioners persist against all common sense, suggest continuing the discussion separately to protect the limited time available to everyone – the facilitator should intervene to suggest that anyway, and will probably support a suggestion to move on! Do make a note of the organisation that the questioner represents, so that you can find out afterwards what underlies this apparent lack of understanding.

If you haven't had the opportunity to deliver a presentation during the meeting, ask the meeting's facilitator to circulate your brief Project summary and contact details via email to the network's members afterwards. (If you have delivered a presentation there, you can ask that your PowerPoint slides and accompanying notes, with your contact details, be circulated). Receiving your project summary as an email is useful for those that weren't at the meeting, and a reminder for those that were.

After you've attended a few meetings, you'll find that you'll be able to judge with some accuracy whether subsequent ones are going to be time well spent, or not. Look at the topic areas on the agenda, and which organisation each speaker represents. If the facilitator has copied in all attendees on an email invitation, look at the organisations that have been invited. And once you can gauge their usefulness or otherwise to your Project, you'll have the confidence to 'cherry pick'. So, initially, yes, go to everything – it's a good idea to get your face and your Project known, and a relevant group or organisation may have kindly facilitated this invitation for you. And you want to be included in every relevant emailing list. Ultimately though, you could spend your entire time just going to meetings. If it doesn't look useful to you, in the light of your experience of attending a few meetings, then just politely inform the facilitator that you cannot attend, and request copies of the minutes and copies of any presentations, fact sheets etc. that feature in the meeting. If you see something relevant to your Project in the subsequent attachments, ask the meeting's facilitator to forward on an email from you to that organisation's representative (if you cannot have their direct contact details).

You do need to remember – in every conversation that you have – to maintain the aspects of your Project that are 'set in stone' for you and your committee. Otherwise a treehouse becomes a swing.

Presentations within meetings

In presentations to organisations, remember to focus on com-municating: who, what, when, where, how and why. In addition to this core information, each presentation that you deliver should be tailored to the audience – i.e. how they can help you, and how you can help them.

PowerPoint slides are an effective way to deliver your information concisely and memorably (see below). If you're not confident with the mechanics of preparing your slides, a fellow committee member, friend or family member may be able to help. (There are also step-by-step guides on the internet.)

PowerPoint Presentations – the nitty-gritty

- You could send the PowerPoint slides to the meeting's facilitator ahead of time, so that you don't have to worry about 'sharing your screen' etc. when it gets to your turn on the day. You can also do this before face-to-face meetings. Either way, the facilitator will happily move your slides along at a signal from you

- Ask in advance whether your presentation could be first up on the list of items on the agenda. Otherwise – and it happens to us all sometimes – your anticipatory nerves may mean that you miss an important comment or piece of information from the discussions. You'll probably get more focused attention from attendees the closer you are to the top of the agenda too. Don't worry about how you'll be perceived for asking – just explain that you're a little nervous. In network meetings it's not usually important who speaks first – it's not like being a 'keynote speaker' at a conference

- For virtual meetings, the facilitator will send you a meeting link beforehand, so all you'll need to do is click on it a couple of minutes before the start time. (Do have the facilitator's phone number / email address to hand though in case of technical hiccups, and that of the admin person for the organisation hosting the meeting.) You might spend the minutes before the start time in a virtual 'waiting room', with a message that reads 'The host will invite you in when the meeting has started' or similar

- If you can't summarise all the information for your presentation in five to seven minutes (and certainly within the time stipulated by the facilitator), trim it until you can, while not losing sight of your main points, i.e. who, what, when, where, how, why

- Don't read off the PowerPoint slides – it demonstrates lack of preparation, and it's quite irritating (I can't be the only person in the room wanting to shout 'I can read!'). It might feel like a useful tool if you're nervous, but it would be much better to have slides that pique interest without being too 'busy' visually, with attention-grabbing headlines relevant to your Project (such as '14% of school children in the UK don't eat breakfast', '347 playgrounds in England have closed since 2014') and prompt cards that give you reminders, so that you expand on what's written on the slides. Be clear and precise

- Prompt cards will help even if you're very familiar with the subject – nerves can get in the way, or a question can throw you off a little

- Accompanying photos will speak a thousand words, and be recalled better than any text: people won't take too much new verbal information in

- If your presentation is to a group of professionals, you won't need to go into too much detail about the current situation for your service users. Demonstrate awareness, based on your research

- Emphasise that your purpose is not to duplicate work, but rather to add value

- Always think positively when writing the content of your presentations. You are setting up something that will contribute to alleviating problems for your service users. Focus on how you're going to be doing that

- Attention spans are short: deliver a brief, well-rounded presentation, focusing on key points. And you might want your final slide to be a quick summary of what you've said, with your contact details

- Ask that your presentation be circulated to the network members with your accompanying notes. And, for face-to-face presentations, have short handouts outlining your Project, and again include your contact details

- You should be able to anticipate the majority of questions too: they will be based on the six questions outlined in chapter 1 – which your research and relevant communications will enable you to answer. There may also be comments based on perceived threats to other local groups' resources or funding, which you will need to address (briefly and clearly) for everyone present. You should draft brief answers to all these beforehand, so that all the information that you might need is to hand. There will be some questions that you won't know the answer to – acknowledge this and say that you'll get back to them (within a stipulated, short time period, certainly within a week) with a response – and do so. You may also learn new information – perhaps there is a grassroots service that you were previously unaware of – which you should gratefully acknowledge and incorporate into your research

- You waited ages to get this slot and you did the preparation: don't let the technology get in your way. In case the tech goes wrong in a face-to-face presentation, have a back-up – copies of your slides with the accompanying notes to distribute, and a two minutes' summary of the main points that you could say with only reference to brief notes (don't just read aloud with your head down –

it'll seem interminable, and you may lose your audience). I say two minutes as, without seeing the bullet points and accompanying colourful images, it can be difficult to hold peoples' attention after that time. Have the same summary to hand for virtual presentations too, in case the tech goes wrong, and assure everyone that you'll be asking the facilitator to circulate your slides and accompanying notes.

It won't go perfectly, and that's fine

Things will never go perfectly, ever, so don't expect them to. Do take steps to make sure that hiccups are the things outside your control – e.g. technical issues for virtual presentations, or, for in-person meetings, the noise from the group in the next room etc. You can practise delivering your presentation to people in your own circle of family and friends. You may, for example, want to time how long it takes you to deliver this presentation, and perhaps consciously slow down your pace of speaking. That's certainly one that I always need to do – if I don't practise it out loud to someone first, timing it etc., and then subsequently keep an eye on the time as I deliver the presentation, then I am more likely to speak too quickly. If you're delivering this in person rather than virtually, you may need to practise projecting your voice.

Nerves

If you feel a little nervous, that's okay. It's nerve-wracking. You're doing something important. But the more you prepare – e.g. timing your delivery, and rewriting and editing the presentation until the message is clear and concise – the less nervous you'll be. Every person in the meeting will be able to identify with presentation nerves, however experienced they are. Believe you can do it – and just a few minutes later you'll be able to relax.

Don't be negative or critical

Not out loud anyway! Don't talk negatively about people or organisations who were no help at all. Not just because that's mean-spirited, but because they may help with something else in the future, and crucially because the Third Sector is as rife with gossip as any other working environment, and discretion is always highly valued. (There's something to be said for the old adage 'If you have nothing good to say, then say nothing'.) And you might just have met them on a really bad day – it happens. It's not about blame, but about achieving the best outcome for your Project.

For example, I was talking to a representative of an organisation, and this person was adamant that the Project under discussion wasn't wanted or needed – although I had ample evidence that it was – and they further insisted that their service was an exact match. This was like saying 'Hmmm, chalk and cheese – well, both are great on toast'. I was unfailingly polite, merely gently pointing out the need, and how and in what ways their service differed. Afterwards this person sent me an email saying '...there's room for both Projects and if I can help in any way let me know'. That was the only aspect of my communications with that organisation that I shared with others.

Do also give credit where it's due: it's always appreciated, and will usually be repaid to you a thousand-fold.

There may be some representatives of local groups that you don't want involved in your Project.

And that's okay – it's your Project. You can say 'no', politely, to any person or group that you feel is trying to steer you away from the aims of your Project, or who is driven by their own vested interests... Just politely reiterate your plan, and touch upon the need highlighted in your research. These groups and organisations will be among the gate-keepers of potential service users for your Project. If you don't play nicely – and regrettably, through no fault of your own, sometimes even if you do – it's possible that people who would otherwise benefit from your Project won't hear about it.

Signposting

Whatever the premise of your Project, you'll want to be able to effectively 'signpost' or direct your service users to further help and support within the community. That's another reason for your exhaustive research into what services are currently operating in your area of interest, and for working with local groups. For accurate and useful signposting you'll need to keep in regular contact with the organisations that you're referring service users to – probably every couple of months. This is for a number of reasons:

- You'll then be sure that the opening hours and indeed the scope of the organisation or group remains accurate

- You'll have up-to-date contact information – phone numbers occasionally change, organisations move offices, and people will change jobs – and you're very unlikely to be updated as to changes if you're not in touch regularly

- You're demonstrating partnership-working, which is appreciated by both the local organisations themselves and by funders

- You can check whether each organisation still wants referrals, or if they have a backlog / are operating a waiting list etc.

- Your records are reflecting signposting as a further accomplishment by your Project for your Reports to Funders and (fellow) committee members

- The statistics will be good content for your periodic e-newsletter to the local Community, the group's Facebook page etc.

JO'S STORY: MID-MARCH

Jo contacted Tall Town CVS, and the Community Worker there, Pavel, was pleased to hear about the planned initiative. He explained that while the local Council monitored, facilitated and sometimes gave financial support to the work of the Third Sector in Tall Town, it did not directly deliver services. He gave Jo the contact details for Amy, who facilitated the local Food Insecurity Network, and for Clive, the manager of a charity that ran the largest independent foodbank in the area. Pavel said that when the time came for Jo to recruit volunteers, he would advertise the Project's volunteering roles. He did mention that some areas of the town struggled to attract volunteers, and mentioned Biddlevale in particular.

Through her research, Jo had already identified 'Love Tall Town', a volunteer-led group involved in coordinating food-related provision across the town, and she had their advertised email address and phone number. Jo reached out to Clive, Amy and to 'Love Tall Town'.

The manager of the large foodbank, Clive, was very supportive of the proposed Project. He gave Jo the current picture in terms of not-for-profit food provision in the town, and suggested a couple of areas that he felt could benefit particularly from the service – Tymbown and Foutlin – the latter of which Clive said featured a great deal of hidden poverty. He gave Jo the contact details for the person managing a Community Centre in Tymbown. Clive invited Jo to the next quarterly Foodbank Network meeting, which was eight weeks away. Clive explained that it was made up of both local foodbanks and community pantries, and that it was separate to the Food Insecurity Network which Clive also attended. Jo asked if she could give a brief overview of the Family Dining Project at the

Foodbank Network meeting, and Clive said that he'd introduce her to the facilitator, Matt.

Clive spoke with Jo about his foodbank's experience of accessing surplus food locally, and that of other not-for-profit providers, basically that it was no longer freely available in the town and that, even with paying a monthly subscription for weekly surplus food deliveries from the local distributing organisation, they'd probably need to buy food from local supermarkets to supplement their supplies. He also said that if Jo's Project ran twice a week, they would need to think about either sourcing two separate food deliveries (so increasing the cost), or finding somewhere to store the food that would meet with the approval of the Council's Environmental Health department. Jo was concerned about these unanticipated costs, but felt that her research would prove persuasive to funders as to the need for and the positive impact of her twice-weekly Project. She did reflect though that aiming to open every weekday during the school holidays might be too ambitious when the Project was starting off, with the potentially time-consuming work that might be needed to adhere to food safety legislations related to food storage, and the added costs that might be difficult for a new and unproven Project to secure. She was also conscious of Pavel's comment about volunteer recruitment, and felt that it might be sensible to start small and build the service gradually.

END OF MARCH:

Jo was unable to reach Matt from the Foodbank Network by phone, and he had not responded to her initial email after a week. Jo asked Clive to introduce her to Matt via email, forwarding on her email to Matt too, and Matt subsequently responded promptly. He said that the Foodbank Network meetings were quite informal, and that she could have four or five minutes to speak about her Project at the next meeting (scheduled for mid-May). Matt said that after the meeting he would happily disseminate any information that Jo wanted to circulate. Jo was initially concerned that this might cause a delay to the Project, but she had the contact details of all the local not-for-profit food providers from the Council's Directory of Services, including foodbanks and community pantries, and knew that she could still approach them individually.

Jo contacted all the not-for-profit food providers listed on the Council's website, utilising either direct introductions from Clive, Amy or Sunil, or mentioning the relationship as a first sentence. The response was still a little disappointing, despite her gentle persistence – about 35% – but this enabled Jo to establish relationships with at least those few representatives from relevant organisations and groups, to find out what provision consisted of, where it ran from, how often etc., and to get some hints and tips: for example, Jo learned that offering volunteers the opportunity to eat alongside the families would make the role even more attractive, as many local people were struggling with the cost of eating healthily. Jo also learned that providing training opportunities was attractive to many volunteers, and that anyway the Project's lead volunteers would need to undergo food safety training. Jo made a note to find out how this could be accessed, and how much it would cost. She decided that she would revisit the 65% of groups that hadn't responded when the Project was about to begin, asking them to signpost their service users to the Project, and meanwhile would periodically keep the 35% who had responded up-to-date with progress.

After contacting Amy from the Food Insecurity Network, Jo was invited to attend their next meeting. It was arranged as a virtual meeting, and it was to be held the next day. It was too late to include Jo on the agenda as a speaker, but she had the opportunity to speak very briefly about her Project during the initial introductions at the meeting, as everyone did. (Appendix A shows the presentation that Jo might have delivered had she been given the opportunity at this stage.) Jo had already planned and practised her under-a-minute introduction, and though nervous she delivered it clearly: 'Hi. I'm Jo Stead, Chair of the Family Dining Charity. We're working to set up free communal hot meals provision for local families who are not in a position to eat regularly or healthily. I'd welcome an opportunity to learn from you as to what provision there is currently in Tall Town**, and where we could best make a difference. I'll put my contact details in the Chat, and would really like to hear from you.' Jo then put her name, title (i.e. Chair), Project name, and contact details in the Chat, with the request that people contact her so that she could answer any questions about the Project, and find out about existing and planned provision in the area.

At the meeting, Jo was asked a question by a provider of low-cost microwaveable meals locally: 'How are you helping people to learn to manage their money [i.e. encouraging 'financial resilience'] if you give the food away free?' This was accompanied by nods of support from a councillor representing a relatively affluent area of the town, and demonstrated to Jo that free meals provision wasn't a universally welcomed idea. Jo's research enabled her to point out that 65% of local families were receiving benefits either to supplement a low income or because of worklessness, and that a further 10% were not eligible to receive any financial help at all because of their immigration status. Jo stated very reasonably that no amount of budgeting advice would help stretch a severely limited or non-existent budget. She also pointed out the extra benefits of the Project in terms of health and wellbeing, as the meals would be eaten communally, in a safe and supportive environment. Jo could also have spoken about the prohibitive cost of the utilities required to prepare meals, and – for some people – the lack of knowledge about cooking food from scratch, but she decided to hold back unless that person posed a follow-up question, as the rest of the participants would be familiar with all these reasons.

During the Food Insecurity Network meeting, Jo learned about the Government's Holiday Activities and Food Programme (HAF), and thought that while that initiative was running it might be unnecessary for her Project to extend their service during the school holidays anyway.

After the meeting, Amy agreed to circulate a few lines about the Family Dining Project that Jo had prepared, along with her contact details, to the group's membership. Shortly after this,

Jo was contacted by a Public Health Practitioner, Parminder, from the local Council, who had been at the Food Insecurity Network meeting and wanted to know more about the Project and to offer any help that was appropriate. Parminder gave Jo a great deal of useful advice and guidance in terms of areas of greatest need, reaffirming both Jo's research and the information that she'd already learned from speaking with Pavel and Clive, and from listening to the Network meeting participants. Parminder promised to signpost the Project to potential service users when it was up and running. Jo offered to keep Parminder up-to-date with the work of the Family Dining Project, and to share the results of their Monitoring and Evaluation work, which Parminder said would be warmly appreciated.

The volunteer coordinating the work of 'Love Tall Town', Sunil, picked up Jo's phone message and subsequent email after a few days, and contacted her. After hearing more about the Project, he promised to publicise it when it was up and running. Sunil also suggested that Biddlevale might not be practical in terms of volunteer recruitment, as the local residents had resisted all efforts to involve them in initiatives over the last few years. This had also been mentioned by Pavel of Tall Town CVS. Sunil suggested that Jo might want to contact the Council's Public Health department, but said that he had no contact details to give her. Jo knew that, had Parminder from Public Health not kindly reached out to her already, Clive or Amy would have been able to give her that information, or Pavel from CVS. Sunil also mentioned 'Families Support in the Sunvale Borough', a charity supporting families across the borough within which Tall Town was located. He provided Jo with the contact details of that charity's community worker, Sarah.

MID-APRIL:

The facilitator of the Food Insecurity network meeting, Amy, was a Community Development Officer with the local Housing Association – a not-for-profit organisation with much social housing stock in the town (but the facilitator could equally have been from the local Council or from a charitable organisation.

Wherever they are from, they should have the local map of provision, and local contacts, at their fingertips). Amy was happy to meet with Jo separately, and proved very helpful, suggesting two of the same venues that had already been recommended to her (located in Trulegate), so Jo would be able to approach those venues with introductions from local organisations, if that was decided by her and her Committee to be the best area for the Project. Being close to the town centre, Jo knew that Trulegate would also make travel for volunteers – and for those service users who were not within walking distance, and could afford the bus fare – more straightforward. Amy invited Jo to give a brief presentation (up to ten minutes' duration) at the next Food Insecurity Network meeting, which would be held two months later and which would be face-to-face rather than virtual. Jo gratefully accepted.

Jo reached out to Sarah from 'Families Support in the Sunvale Borough', who Sunil from Love Tall Town had given her the contact details for. Sarah proved a little difficult to get hold of – she covered a large area for her under-resourced organisation, and worked part-time. After some persistence though, Jo got the opportunity to speak with Sarah, who explained the support and help that her organisation was able to provide to local families, and in which areas of the town. Sarah felt that the Family Dining Project would be of huge benefit to local families, suggesting that Biddlevale was most in need, but admitting that they'd never been able to get anything running there over a long period. Jo asked if that was because volunteers were difficult to attract, and Sarah said that this had been the main issue. Sarah did suggest though that their social media-led recruitment drive may have excluded many people who had no access to the internet. She said that a more grassroots approach might work better, but agreed with Jo that this would be time-consuming and quite possibly still unproductive.

Sarah provided an introduction to Beth, a support worker at a local charity providing practical help to refugees. Jo contacted Beth, explaining that Sarah Woods from 'Families Support in the Sunvale Borough' had kindly given her Beth's details.

Beth was warmly supportive of Jo's work, and said that many refugee families could benefit. Beth asked whether there would be a vegetarian option at the community meals, as many of the people she supported either ate no meat or would need it to be sourced from a particular supplier and / or prepared in a particular way. Jo said that was something that had not occurred to her, but that she would chat with the committee and get back to Beth.

By mid-April, and in time for that month's Committee meeting, Jo had learned from the Community partners that, of the three areas being considered, Tymbown was actually rated among the most deprived in Europe, and consequently this had received a great deal of funding, and was becoming well-resourced – and though the feeling from the local community is that these resources may not have been targeted entirely appropriately, or with sufficient involvement from potential beneficiaries, nevertheless further funding would be difficult to attract. Another, Biddlevale, has demonstrated very little community involvement in any local initiatives over the last few years, and the suggestion is that this would make a Project that relies on local volunteers difficult to sustain. However, Trulegate had a strong sense of community cohesion, and useful locally-led initiatives tended to flourish. There were a number of food banks, and two community pantries (in which members can pick and buy groceries at about a third of the usual retail price). Also, although there is a 'pay what you can' Community Café, in which people pay what they can afford, and a soup kitchen for rough sleepers provided by a faith-based organisation, there is no free communal meals provision for families. (This was also true of the rest of the town, as Jo's initial research had indicated.) The food banks and food pantries in Trulegate are still well-supported by local volunteers, though numbers had understandably dropped when many local workers returned to work after being furloughed during the Covid lockdowns. This area also has several 'Houses of Multiple Occupancy' (HMOs), within which homeless families, some of whom have

'No Recourse to Public Funds', live in cramped conditions with few if any cooking facilities. Jo already knew that Trulegate neighbours a more affluent area with comfortably-off retirees in good health, and that many of the local university students live close by. Jo thought that both factors may make it an additional source of committed volunteers.

The committee agreed with Jo that Trulegate seemed the ideal location for the Family Dining Project.

Jo discussed with the Committee the idea of a vegetarian option for inclusivity, though she hadn't herself envisaged having two main courses. She found that, understandably, no-one wanted the complication of preparing two separate main meals. Geoff said that many people expected to see meat in a meal. Pete, who managed a café, said that using meat or fish greatly increased the Environmental Health safeguards that would need to be taken into account, and that this seemed unfair to ask of a volunteer-led team. Naomi pointed out that there were lots of meat-substitute sausages, mince, etc on the market, and that these could be used if the exclusively vegetarian meals proved unpopular. And she added that vegetarian meals would be much cheaper to produce. After some discussion, Jo and the committee decided to offer one main course as originally planned, and the majority of the committee members agreed that making that a vegetarian meal was the best option.

The committee discussed whether they should begin by running their service once a week rather than twice, because in addition to the hours needed by committed volunteers with the twice-weekly meal, they had not anticipated the complications (and costs) inherent in sourcing and possibly transporting and storing food for a second weekly service. Pete, the committee member in the catering industry, advised them of the many regulations around the safe storage of food, which they would need to stringently adhere to if they decided to have just one weekly surplus food delivery and then store half for the second meals service of the week, including providing a food storage facility approved by the Environmental Health Department, as Clive had mentioned. It was suggested that the food for the second service of the week could instead be bought from supermarkets at the retail price, though some committee members had been attracted to using only surplus food which would otherwise go into landfill, and it also meant more volunteer time would be used in picking and transporting the food, and there would be mileage costs. This all meant an increased environmental impact too.

Jo was adamant that with the huge need in the area, providing two communal meals a week was a minimum. It was felt though that it would be too much to coordinate and resource buying food from supermarkets once a week for everything that they'd need to feed perhaps fifteen or twenty families or more, while the Project was becoming established. It was agreed that, for the first year at least, they would run twice a week as planned, and would need two surplus food deliveries each week, on the day of each meals service. It was further decided that any fresh food not used in the meals would be offered free to a local community pantry, so that there would be no waste. However, the committee decided that, for at least the first year of their Project, it would not be feasible to increase their communal meals service to extend to every weekday during the holidays, as Jo had initially envisaged. It was felt that it might be something to consider after the conclusion of the Government's HAF initiative, once the Project was well-established, and if they had the support from local volunteers and from funders to do this.

Jo and a couple of members of the Committee (including the Health and Safety lead) arranged to visit the two venues in Trulegate that seemed most promising. Both had a five star hygiene rating for their semi-commercial kitchens, so that when it came to registering with the Council's Environmental Health Department they knew that they would have a good foundation for the service. The committee members had hoped that the venues would provide their facilities free of charge, but the cost of utilities, and the loss of revenue for venues during the COVID lockdowns, made that unlikely. Both venues though had similar hire rates, with a reduction for registered charities.

Both had a little space for the Project to store their pasta and rice, and their tinned goods, so that it would not have to be transported to and from the venue. However, only one would be available in late afternoon every week on the same two weekdays, having capacity around their regular bookings from Scout groups, 'Parents and Toddlers' groups, etc.

(**Mid-April** – fundraising begins – see chapter 7)

MID-MAY:

By the date of the Foodbank Network meeting that Clive had invited Jo to, she was in a position to give a specific overview of the Family Dining charity in the five minutes allocated to her – how exactly it would deliver a service in the first year, and where. She asked that – once sufficient funding was confirmed – the representatives of the foodbanks and community pantries would spread the word about the service to their own customers. All were happy to do so, and Matt, the facilitator, said that he'd forward on Jo's good news (with e-leaflets) to everyone in the network, when she contacted him.

END OF MAY:

At the second Food Insecurity Network meeting that Jo attended, her presentation was well received. Because she had been speaking with local groups and organisations in the two months since the previous meeting, she was able to update everyone as to who she had spoken with and the progress that had been made. (The slides and accompanying notes from Jo's presentation are in Appendix B.) During this second meeting, the Network members also discussed Warm Spaces, and Jo subsequently spoke with her committee (at their mid-June meeting) about registering the Project as a Warm Space for families to attend: this required no additional facilities as the venue would be heated throughout the duration of the Project anyway, and would mean that the Project would be listed on the Council's website and signposted even more widely. This was felt to be a good idea.

ENDNOTES

* Later on, if / when you're considering venues, this provides one of many opportunities to think about the dignity of your service users: for example, more and more people are having to access food banks to feed their families. But no-one wants to be seen queuing outside. So, you'd want to avoid opening it by a bus stop or on a main road (and you wouldn't want to start your sessions until after the morning commute has finished).

** Jo specified the area of interest because many attendees will be responsible for a larger area than the town – possibly having a borough-wide remit.

1. Joe Navarro's 'The Dictionary of Body Language' (2018), published by Thorson

7

FUNDRAISING

You might be wondering why you'd need to raise funds, especially if you're part of a small group of committed volunteers and you're all giving your time for free. But there are going to be costs for your Project from the beginning – not least equipment and possibly venue hire – and you wouldn't want to limit membership of your committee or your volunteer group to those who are not only committed, caring and hardworking but who also have the money to fund their travel costs, and to chip in for insurance, publicity materials etc. So it's time to turn your attention to getting the resources that you will need to deliver this Project cost-effectively and sustainably. This chapter concerns the practicalities of raising funds to get your Project up and running, and also provides funding avenues that you could utilise throughout the duration of your Project.

Make clear to funders the professional way in which you have set up your project; this will help to reassure any funder that their grant is safe in your hands, and that you will deliver on your plans. Be realistic: small is beautiful, at least initially, as well as being practical and manageable. Growth must be knowledge-based: knowledge of the Third Sector, of funding streams, and crucially of what you can do and what you need to do in relation to the needs of your service users in the short and longer term – which you'll learn first-hand while you're delivering your Project. It takes time, work and research, and you need to give yourself and your team the space to learn.

The UK Government has written a very accessible guide to the dos and don'ts of charity fundraising, and I've cited it as 'Further Reading' for you at the end of this chapter.

What exactly will you need this initial funding for?

Get together as a group, and think about what you are going to need in order to deliver your service effectively during the first year of your Project. Itemise the resources that you'll require – one-off costs like equipment, plus venue hire if necessary, insurance, utilities, phone contracts etc. Get several quotes where appropriate. As far as possible, try to anticipate what you'll need when you've been up and running for a while and are perhaps at capacity, because your needs in terms of resources on day three will be different from those needs on day 300. Funders may each cover different aspects of your Project's costs, and you're likely to need to apply to several. And bear in mind that costs related to your volunteers will be an essential part of your fundraising application: funders will recognise how important it is to look after your volunteers. So include costs related to volunteers' recruitment, their expenses, and relevant training courses, as well as the cost of a fun event to say 'thank you'.

What you will be asked, and what you need to say

Usually, the size of the donation that you're applying for will be reflected in the number of questions and / or the depth of information that you need to provide in a grant application – so an application for a few hundred pounds would require relatively little from your group, while larger pots of money would tend to need more detailed information. Be guided by the word-count given for each question, and if possible use your entire word allocation (though do not exceed it): you will have a great deal of relevant information to draw on from your meticulous research, and you will be given a 'score' for every point covered on the funder's checklist. The work that you have done to build relationships with relevant local organisations will also come to the fore here. Think of each funding application as an opportunity, not as a test: it's an opportunity for the funder to understand your Project and to recognise the difference that you'll be making, and to want to play a part in achieving that.

It is best to start answering your application form in a Word document so that you can edit or expand your answers – then just 'cut and paste' these into the on-line form. (Some funders may offer a paper form, too.) I'd recommend that you have a look at the National Lottery's 'Awards for All' application form, or their 'Reaching Communities' form for a good idea of what you'll be asked. Beside each of the questions on these forms is an explanation of what they are looking for in your answers, with examples and word limits.

The questions from other funders may be a little less obvious at first glance, or their application form may not present as many opportunities to let the funder know about your service in-depth – usually those with only relatively small grants at their disposal. I've listed below a guide to 'typical' questions, i.e. what funders are looking for in your answers. And if the application form instead gives you one main question to tell the funder about your Project in some depth – for example, Asda's Empowering Local Communities Grant application form asks 'Please tell us what you will use this money for' (250 words limit) – then the questions below will serve as a useful framework for your answer.

What would you like to do?

The funder is expecting you to describe the aims of your Project: for example, 'We want to increase the skills of young school refusers', or 'We want to help older isolated people to engage in social activities.'

What difference will your project make?

Funders attach a lot of importance to making a difference to people. These differences are also known as 'outcomes', and your answer will need to demonstrate positive change, such as 'reducing loneliness' or 'improving well-being'. For example, older people's mobility will increase; or their mental health will improve; or a health condition will be managed better; younger people will gain skills that will make them more employable etc. And list here the activities that the grant will pay for, e.g. 'We will hold three dance sessions every month' or 'we'll run six training sessions every quarter'. You can demonstrate the difference that your Project will make using your research findings.

Who will benefit from it?

Be as precise as you can, e.g. young people aged sixteen to twenty-five, or people over fifty years of age. Give the number of people that you anticipate will take up your service as accurately as possible – you could base your estimate on previous work by your group or others. Don't inflate numbers – funders want to see that you've thought about the numbers and given your best estimate. And don't be tempted to play safe and give yourself too low a number either – you could look expensive to the funder. Emphasise the need in the community, using your knowledge and experience of it, and reassure the funder that your Project won't be taken over by those who are not in need.

If you are successful with your grant and then find, for example, that you are not reaching the numbers you predicted, make sure you understand why this has happened. Utilise your Monitoring and Evaluation processes (chapter 12) to ascertain what the underlying issue is – and whether you could find ways to address this so that you 'catch up' over the year, or whether it is for example related to addressing the more complex and time-consuming needs of perhaps a smaller group of people. Let your funder know – show them that you fully understand the workings of your Project and your Community.

How long do you expect to run it for?

You'll often be asked for a start date, which can be an estimate. Take a look at each funder's website and see how long it will take them to give you a decision, and where possible build this anticipated time period into your plans. But if you're planning on running, for example, a summer play-scheme and a particular funder wouldn't be letting you know their decision until September, do still put down the start date that's right for you; you'll be spreading your net in terms of your funding search anyway, and you never know. Usually initial grants are given for work that will be delivered over a year (not less as funders do not think you will make a difference in a very short time).

How will you make sure people know about it?

Here the funder wants to know how you will run your publicity to effectively reach your target group. Social media is the norm but they will want you to also think about those who are digitally excluded, such as rough sleepers and many older people. (See chapters 8 and 10 on the promotion of your service.) And include here the community-based organisations that you have a relationship with, as they will be promoting your Project to their own service users.

How do you plan to learn from it, and to use this learning to shape future projects?

This is where you'd draw on your plans for monitoring and evaluation (chapter 12). Funders are always keen to know how you will find out that the services you deliver have made a difference.

Is it something new, or are you continuing something that has worked well previously?

When your Project is no longer new, this question will be an opportunity to renew your existing work and add areas of expansion (if appropriate) that you've identified in your monitoring and evaluation (see chapter 12).

Where's the money coming from?

Make sure that you meet the specific criteria for a grant for the funder that you're applying to. Otherwise they will be unable to consider your application.

- **Your local Council** will either have funds themselves to distribute to the Community projects and services that match their current initiatives, or they will be working with a community-based organisation to administer and support this. Speak with the Council's 'Grants Officer' or 'Community Development Officer' or similarly named person

- **Contact your local CVS** – They'll know if an organisation administers money on behalf of the Council, and will have the relevant contact details. The CVS will also circulate regular funding opportunity updates, so do sign up for their e-newsletter etc. They also promote (and often run) free training seminars on fundraising

- **Local, Parish or Town Councils** – Despite the wording, 'Parish' doesn't refer to the local Church's resources. These are the first level of local government, and can give grants to local groups who fit their criteria

- **Awards for All (England)** – Lottery* funding, for funding between £300 and £10,000, for up to one year. This is for voluntary and community organisations, and must involve local people and support local communities

- **Veolia** – Grants of between £10,000 and £75,000 to create or improve buildings or outside spaces for the benefit of the community

- **Asda Foundation** – including their Empowering Local Communities Grant of between £500-£1500 for a year

- **Fund-raising from faith-based organisations** – e.g. Churches (especially during Lent), Mosques (not least during Ramadan) and Temples may be a further source of funds

- **Local Lions Clubs, Soroptimist Clubs, Rotary Clubs and the associated Inner Wheels** are also a potential source of funds for your Project

- **Reaching Communities (England)** – from the National Lottery, awards grants of over £10,000 to charities, voluntary and community groups and social enterprises

- **UK Community Foundations** – look at their website to find your local grant-giving organisation

- **Local businesses** too could be a source of money – many workplaces carry out small-scale fundraising throughout the year for the charity that they've chosen to benefit that year. Look at the websites of your local businesses under 'charitable giving' or 'charitable partnerships' for the opportunities to seek a grant, usually via a simple on-line form. Many businesses also donate in-kind gifts such as equipment (see below for more on in-kind donations)

- **Online fundraising platforms** such as JustGiving – a prominent fundraising platform which enables people to raise money for great causes. (Famously, Captain Sir Tom Moore raised over £32,000,000 to support the NHS through the JustGiving platform.) 'A small processing fee is applied to donations to cover card payments, which is set by external card providers'[1]. And, over the years, more online giving platforms have emerged, such as 'Enthuse', which 'provides an easily customisable fundraising page for charities and competitive platform pricing'[2]

- **You could consider raising funds from individuals through raffles, sales of plants etc.** A successful sale could raise about £200 profit. And while we're on the subject of cash: if a group of people are literally giving you a bag of cash that they have kindly raised for your Project, bring someone with you from your group to collect it, and count it in the presence of that person. I picked up a very generous donation once from a group of kindly civil servants, and when I got home found that it was £30 light on the amount written on the envelope. I don't doubt that this was an administrative error, or that my employing charity would have attached no blame to me. But nevertheless I felt that I had to put the £30 in.

Funding databases:

- Charity Excellence Framework – a free service. As well as providing a directory of trusts and foundations, it also has links to hundreds of other free grant funding databases and online funder lists

- My Funding Central – Free annual subscription while your turnover is under £30,000, and very reasonable indeed after that

- Grants Online – relatively reasonable one-person sub-scription cost. You can 'search for grants from Trusts & Foundations, and the UK Government Lottery'.

Restricted funds

While donations from individuals are 'unrestricted' and can be spent or saved in line with your aims, a grant is 'restricted' to the purpose you gave for needing it. So it must be used for precisely the purpose that you've stipulated, and within the agreed time-frame. Using the funds for a different purpose will result in you having to return the money.

Many years ago, I spent a year on secondment working with the volunteer-led committee of a Community group. As part of my role, I secured funding to support children with disabilities in local Summer Play-schemes. The committee decided to spend that money on something unrelated to this – incidentally, on something which would benefit the members comprising the decision-making committee. My explanation that this is just not how funding works was dismissed with the comment 'What are they going to do? Take it back?!' Well, yes. I notified the funder, who demanded that the money be returned immediately and in full.

Any unspent money would need to be returned to the funder at the end of the period of time covered by the funding, so do keep an eye on that throughout the period of funding – i.e. make sure that it's all spent (appropriately)!

Just a note on in-kind donations

The funders may expect you to 'show willing' with a proportionally small contribution from your Project. The good news is that this isn't necessarily cash: in-kind donations from local companies such as equipment, or their staff's expertise (e.g. to provide support with social media etc.) and the time given by your volunteers, count towards this too. Gifts from supermarkets and stores for raffles or sales would also come under the heading of 'gifts-in-kind'.

Applying to several potential funders simultaneously

You'll probably be applying to several funders simultaneously for grants to support the same aspects of your Project; fundraising can be a time-consuming process, and the likelihood is that not all of your applications will be successful, so you need to spread your net widely. If you are lucky, though, and are offered two pots of funding for the same aspect of your Project, you can always ask one of those funders to defer their grant to the next year.

Some of your funding applications may be turned down

As intimated above, it might be that one or more of your funding applications is turned down. This isn't a judgement on your Project: every funder will receive many more applications than they could possibly fund, so you should expect some rejections. Always request feedback; it'll be invaluable both for reapplying to that particular funder and for other funding applications. Your tone for this should be humble: 'Where did we go wrong?' Never argue – it won't change the decision (they've just followed their own processes) and it reflects poorly on your Project. It may also mean that you're looked upon less favourably the following year when you need repeat funding (and when you've addressed the issue highlighted in their feedback).

The next stage: fundraising when your Project is up and running

After your Project has been running for about five or six months** you can begin to approach your existing funders (depending on their remit), and apply to appropriate new sources of funding, for money to support your Project in subsequent years (typically one to three years). Fundraising is something that should be in the committee's minds regularly throughout each year, because you'll have two distinct funding processes running in tandem: on the one hand you'll be using your Monitoring and Evaluation processes (chapter 12) to justify your current funding, gathering the evidence required to demonstrate the positive difference that your Project is making within your community for sufficient numbers of vulnerable or marginalised people living locally, and showing that you're on track to achieve your realistic targets etc; and on the other hand you'll also be using your Monitoring and Evaluation processes to look to next year and subsequent years, and deciding whether to maintain your existing provision (though building in the anticipated increases in costs), or to expand upon or even alter the focus of your Project as a result of your research and experience. And whichever future you envisage for your Project, your work to justify and build upon your Project's relationship with existing funders, and to find and cultivate suitable new funders, will be ongoing.

Further reading

Charity Fundraising: a Guide to Trustee Duties CC20 –

- https://www.gov.uk/government/publications/charities-and-fundraising-cc20

  - There are 6 principles for your charity's fundraising: Planning effectively; supervising your fundraisers; protecting your charity's reputation, money and other assets; identifying and ensuring compliance with the laws or regulations that apply specifically to your charity's fundraising; identifying and following any recognised standards that apply to your charity's fundraising; being open and accountable.

JO'S STORY: MID-APRIL:

Jo and the committee now knew the approximate number of families who could benefit from the Family Dining Project (i.e. from the numbers that currently accessed foodbanks and community pantries, though taking into account that this number would be limited by the capacity of their venue), how often the service would run and what precisely it would involve, and what they would need in terms of equipment and venue hire costs. They knew how much a monthly subscription cost for a twice-weekly surplus food delivery from the local supplying organisation would cost, and sensibly allowed for extra money to supplement this food service. They had the support and had received the guidance of many local organisations. As a bonus, they'd even identified a suitable venue. Jo had spoken with her contacts within the Community to ask about food safety training for the committee members and lead volunteers, and had found an organisation willing to include them in their online training, at cost price. It's at this stage that they began the somewhat lengthy process of fundraising. The fundraising sub-committee presented information on all the potential funders that their research had identified, and applications were subsequently submitted to nine funders.

All of the funders approached agreed that the Project was well-researched and well thought-out, and that many of the potential problems had been identified, and practical solutions had been found in the short term to overcome them. It was recognised that suitable processes were planned to monitor and evaluate the Project's impact on the health and wellbeing of local families (see chapter 12), to make the Project sustainable and adaptable to the increasing or changing needs of local families. Within about three months they had received the good news of funding for their twice-weekly communal meals' provision, for twelve months' duration, with a combination of grants from three funders. Jo and the committee knew that after six months of delivering their Project, they would need to begin fundraising to maintain and possibly expand their service (more in chapter 12).

ENDNOTES

* The National Lottery can provide funds ranging from a few hundred pounds to multi-million pound awards. A disadvantage of Lottery funding is that it is seen as money that resulted from gambling, and if you do receive funding from the Lottery this may exclude some potential partners who are ethically opposed to this – e.g. possibly some Faith groups would not want you to use their premises if you'd received Lottery funding.

** Do plan ahead – it can take four to six months to get a decision from prospective funders.

1. https://www.justgiving.com/about/fees

2. https://enthuse.com/

8

GAINING THE SUPPORT OF
THE LOCAL COMMUNITY

You and your committee will need to organise a meeting with people living in the local area. This will enable you to: effectively share information on your Project; promote it; and gain a mix of practical insights and goodwill from local people. These same people will be your main source of volunteers and possibly of service users – directly or indirectly – and perhaps of other resources such as donations of, for example, clothing, food, money etc. In addition they will be a fount of useful knowledge about the local area, and if, for example, someone living next to your prospective venue knows that it floods every third Tuesday, that's useful information. These insights could also prevent you from making a scheduling error: so, for example, you could avoid running a family-friendly Project on the same afternoon as the local parents' weekly get-together – by the ball pool at a fast food restaurant or in a local park – to chat while their children play.

This meeting with the local Community should also tell you: what's been tried before locally; what the Community's understanding is of why it's not running now; and how supportive they would be of your Project in their area. And it's very instructive to find out if there is any opposition to your planned Project, and what that is based on. This gives you an opportunity to clear up misunderstandings. Listening to different viewpoints may enable you to look at aspects of your planned Project from different perspectives too. And some suggestions might simplify a process for you, or point you towards funding or useful partners. Goodwill will come from genuine information-sharing too – from informing the community of all the aspects of the planned Project, asking for information and suggestions, and then listening to them. The goodwill generated may also lead to volunteers, donations etc. too.

This meeting with local people could be either face-to-face or online, depending on your committee's resources and those of the Community. However you choose to run this meeting with local people, the points outlined in this explanation of face-to-face meetings will serve you just as well for online meetings too. These meetings need thought and planning and, unless you and your committee control the process from the get-go, they can otherwise become chaotic and unproductive. This meeting should be supplemented by a discussion section on your committee's Facebook page too, monitored at least every couple of days by your committee's Communications Lead (see chapter 9), so that you can respond in good time to questions and comments, provide updates, and remove inappropriate material.

If online meetings would be practical for you and the local Community, but you'd be boggled by the technical side of running an online session, find out if that expertise exists within your committee, or among your family and friends, or ask any relevant local organisation that you're in touch with if they would facilitate that for you. (This final one would be likely to affect when you could schedule the community meeting, as most organisations keep 'office hours' as far as possible.)

You're not in this alone: your committee should be heavily involved with you in this, and their differing strengths and areas of expertise will really come to the fore here.

The venue

If meeting in person rather than virtually, the meeting should be held on the ground floor of the venue, so that there is access for people with physical disabilities, for parents with children in pushchairs etc. It would be useful to have access to a kitchen at the venue, so you can make the tea and coffee etc. Try to find a venue with facilities for PowerPoint presentations (i.e. a projector to connect your laptop to, and a pull-down screen). You might also want the option to be able to split attendees into smaller groups for post-presentation discussions – either with smaller rooms adjacent to the venue's main hall, or at least with a large enough main room to make it feasible for your smaller groups to speak together without being distracted by everyone else's discussions. Assigning attendees to smaller groups could be due to a number of reasons, including high numbers of attendees (perhaps twenty plus) though that's unlikely; a perceived lack of confidence among attendees in speaking up in larger groups; some potential opposition to the Project that you'd want to dilute; or perhaps the need to find out quite specific information in some depth – such as the quickest or cheapest routes for service users to take to get to the Project. Whether you split your attendees into smaller groups or keep to one large group is a judgement call really that your and the committee will need to make. I have included a section in this chapter to guide you in running these smaller discussion groups, just in case.

There should be an A1 size flipchart pad (and stand) and marker pens at the front of the room (you should be able to hire the stand from the venue). You might be thinking 'What about whiteboards?' But then you're frantically copying down all the comments or suggestions before the board is wiped, rather than having them literally to hand.

Your meeting will probably last up to ninety minutes all in. But when hiring the room, book it for about thirty minutes beyond your advertised finish time – there'll be people still keen to speak with you and the rest of the committee, and clearing up to do.

Promotion of the event

Ask yourself what you want to gain from this meeting. This will need to be built into every aspect of the design and delivery of the event, from the promotion onwards.

Timing-wise, the meeting would usually need to be held on a weekday evening, or on a Saturday, to give people more opportunity to attend. These slots tend to book up fast at venues, so make sure that you have a confirmed booking before you start promoting the meeting! Give yourself about six weeks to promote this locally. This gives people more opportunity to find out about it, and ensures that you have the opportunity to be featured in the monthly newsletters of Third Sector organisations, Parish newsletters etc.

The promotion of the event will need to make clear (very briefly indeed):

- What you are setting out to achieve with your Project

- The benefits of your Project to people living locally

- What you will be asking from the participants in terms of guidance and information.

Make it clear in the promotional literature that you're not providing childcare. Some parents will inevitably need to bring their children along, and because of Safeguarding concerns these children will need to be constantly under that parent's eye. (If a child does become too distractingly boisterous though, you could offer to speak on the phone or in person with the parent instead, at a better time for them.) You could consider providing colouring pencils and paper to keep younger children entertained. Do mention whether there is parking at the venue, and any associated costs for this, and preferably include directions from a notable building or main street, the closest bus routes etc. And mention too in your promotion that your group's Facebook page will outline the learning from the session, along with next steps. Include contact details for the group – a designated email address and phone number. (You'll want contact details specific to your Project – don't use anyone's personal contact details.)

Ask the local groups and organisations that are already aware of the planned Project if they will spread the word through their social media sites and feature it in their next newsletter. Ensure that your committee members spread the word to their local friends and family, and that everyone reaches out to work colleagues through their work intranet, staff noticeboard etc. Ask ward councillors if they could help to promote it through their surgeries and newsletters. Contact your local radio station. Request some coverage on the local paper's website – they are always looking for news. Put promotional posters up well in advance at the venue that's hosting the event – if they are happy for you to do that – and ask that it is featured on their website as an upcoming event. Ask the owners of local coffee shops, newsagents, hairdressers, dentists etc. if you could display a poster promoting the meeting.

For those who cannot attend

It might be that, despite all your work, only a handful of people come along to the meeting and, if so, don't worry at all. People are busy. But that doesn't necessarily mean that they are disinterested – many would still like to know more. They'll have the Project's contact details, and will be able to read the updates on the Facebook page. If they want to learn more or get involved, you're giving them every opportunity. And, because good intentions can fizzle out without a reminder or two, you could provide a quick write-up of the session and of next steps for distribution to the same (social) media outlets that kindly helped you to promote it.

And a quick 'don't' – don't include a local councillor or other notable local person in your meeting, as the focus could swiftly shift from your Project to whatever is going on between them and members of the Community.

What will be the structure of the meeting?

Providing tea and coffee for people on arrival is always welcomed. (And if you're providing biscuits too, keep them in the packets that they came in from the shop – it doesn't look great, but it allows people to check whether they are allergic to any of the ingredients.) Put the drinks and any snacks out in the meeting room itself rather than the corridor or kitchen – it can be difficult to steer people away from the biscuits and into the meeting room otherwise! Have copies of your promotional literature displayed there too – people may want to spread the word themselves, and / or would like a copy of your Project's contact details. Start on time, even if one or two people are still out of their seats – they'll soon sit down. You'll always begin with welcome, thanks and 'housekeeping'. This last one starts with the position of fire exits, and where to assemble if the alarm sounds. The other crucial ones are where the toilets are, and when the tea and coffee will next make an appearance. Then you can begin.

You'll need to deliver a short presentation to outline your Project (see chapter 6 for guidance on presentations). Ten minutes should do it. You'll be addressing people who are genuinely interested in your Project, and possibly one or two who, at first glance, didn't like the sound of it. There may even be one person who's always wanted to set up something completely different but, unlike you, has never done anything about it, who will believe that their hobby horse is finally in the Winner's Circle. This brief opening presentation should provide enough information to satisfy people from the first two categories, and will be sufficiently focused to make Hobby Horse Bob realise that he'll have to pursue his Project idea himself after all.

The presentation is going to have a more informal tone than your presentations to external organisations. You need to 'work the room' differently – you're not so much presenting information as explaining what your and the rest of the committee are trying to do, with the benefit of eye-catching slides. During the presentation:

- Reassure participants that your presentation is only [ ] minutes long (and ask that any questions wait until the end of that time, as the answer might be covered in the information they're about to hear)

- Cover the who, what, why and how of your Project, (bearing in mind that your participants will already know the area, and may be your intended service users)

- Devote one PowerPoint slide to listing the local groups and organisations that you've already spoken with (don't read them off the slide though – just cherry-pick three or four that were particularly useful, and explain why)

- Explain to participants what you want to achieve from the meeting, outlining specifically which areas you would like their support and guidance on

- And then finally give an outline of the session itself: you need to keep the focus of the meeting on furthering the Community's understanding of your Project, and plugging any gaps in your local knowledge as it relates to your service users, your venue, your volunteers and your service delivery. Otherwise the consultation process will be lost in shouted opinions etc.

After the presentation, ask whether anyone has any questions at this stage. Perhaps allow twenty minutes for that. And don't be thrown by questions about something you've literally just covered – just rephrase your previous answer, affably. You wouldn't want to embarrass anyone. I've delivered presentations with the banner of the charity that I was representing behind me, emblazoned with the fact that it's a free service for people aged seventy-five plus, and spent ten minutes emphasising that in a presentation, with photos, illustrative examples etc. And when I got to 'Any questions', I'd be asked, 'How much does it cost?' 'My mum's sixty-four, could she join?'... Patience is a virtue!

After this first Question and Answer session, it's time to address the areas for discussion that you referred to in your presentation. Whether you're speaking with the whole group or smaller break-out groups, your focus will be the same: tackling the gaps in knowledge around venues, resources, sources of volunteers and of service users, learning about grassroots groups that you might not otherwise be aware of etc. You will also be answering questions, recording reactions, and clarifying any misunderstandings that people hold.

Practicalities for break-out groups

If splitting attendees into smaller groups is needed, it would usually follow the first 'Question and Answer' session after your presentation. I have included this because it is better to know how to tackle it and not need it, than to need it and be unsure how to arrange it. And if, in the future, your organisation wants to run workshops, this section will be a useful beginning.

The smaller the group, the easier it is to establish a rapport with people. Ideally you wouldn't have more than about eight to ten people in any one group, though that can be tricky if you're packed to the rafters. (That's not something that I've ever encountered, but we live in hope!) For assigning people to groups, for example, if you've got twenty-seven people, that's about four groups, so maybe indicate each individual and assign them a number one to four. Then ask your group facilitators (i.e. your committee members) to gather their respective people up, and head towards their particular meeting area.

I recently attended one 'community consultation' that allowed each group (comprising twelve people) just fifteen minutes to cover three questions – which is an exercise in futility, and quite possibly a cynical one (the Council running the event was either incompetent or just going through the motions, rather than providing a genuine opportunity to consult local people – that time-frame just doesn't give enough time to properly cover even one question). You'll genuinely want to hear the insights of local people though, so allow enough time for a good discussion. Half an hour should do it – that's enough time for everyone to very briefly introduce themselves within this smaller group (not something you'd ask for in the larger group), and then tackle the subject thoroughly. Each group will need a facilitator to make sure that everyone in the group has the opportunity to contribute, and to keep the group on track – even people obliged to attend meetings for work sometimes need to be tugged back to topic, and your participants aren't being paid!

It might be useful to have two committee members in each group, or a committee member plus a trusted friend; it's difficult to facilitate a discussion and take notes at the same time. The benefits of smaller groups for these discussions are: it allows the committee member acting as facilitator to establish a rapport with this smaller number of attendees; people can introduce themselves, possibly along with a quick ice breaker such as 'what made you smile today?' so that everyone gets to know each other a little more – this will give them more confidence in speaking, sharing their thoughts and asking questions; it's easier to listen to people in small groups, and inter-ruptions are rare; people may possibly come forward to volunteer, or to offer resources; and it's easier to deal with attendees who are too vocal or otherwise disruptive (there's guidance on that below).

Dealing with disruptive attendees

Among the participants there may be someone whose comments are persistently unconstructive, argumentative or just annoyingly distracting. I have been fortunate in not having had to deal with much disruption – perhaps because I'm always giving the good news of a much-needed new local service, as you'll be doing. My husband though says it's because I have the look of a Year Six teacher, which apparently is enough to daunt most potentially disruptive adults! Anyway, I've drawn on some suggestions from a very useful book on workshops here[1], just in case. So, for our purposes: acknowledge the question, say that it's a bit specific or esoteric (or whatever), and / or remind them of the timeline of the event (no-one wants the event to overrun). Then say that you'd be happy to chat with them about it after the meeting (preferably while you're washing up – it's a humanising task, and 'many hands make light work!'). Then you can use this promise of the future discussion to deflect any additional questions from them.

The feedback from the group

After the 30-45 minutes' discussion, break for a cup of tea so that everyone can chat together for 15 minutes, and to allow all the facilitators to compare notes, and because tea has a civilising influence on everyone.

A couple of members of the committee (preferably including you, though you may instead be among those answering additional questions from participants during the break) will need to spend the fifteen minutes' tea break identifying common themes from the group's discussions: popular venue suggestions, details of grassroots groups that you hadn't previously heard about, common questions and misconceptions etc. When you draw all the attendees together for the final twenty minutes or so, you (or another committee member involved in collating the information) would then:

- Summarise the information that you've all gleaned

- Make sure that the relevant questions from attendees have been answered satisfactorily

- Acknowledge kind offers of volunteering time and resources (anonymously – some people are uncomfortable in having their altruism highlighted in public)

- Return to and again dispel any commonly held misconceptions etc.

- Promise to feature a summary of all the information from the event on the group's Facebook page – within, say, two days, along with the next steps. (And, as ever, keep your promise)

- Do mention that anyone who would like to get in touch, whether that's because they have follow-up questions, would like to offer their help, or indeed because they have no access to the internet to read your Facebook page, can phone the mobile number given on the leaflets, and the appropriate member of the committee will get back in touch with them promptly.

Then make eye contact with anyone you've promised to speak with after the event, say you'll be with them momentarily, and thank everyone for coming along and for their invaluable help. If it looks like it might be necessary to further encourage movement to the exit, say that you've only booked the room until— and you don't want to be charged more / keep the caretaker waiting. Ultimately I might say 'Time, gentlemen, please' just because everyone knows that means that the session is finished, and it tends to raise a wry smile among predominantly female participants. Gather the cups up and head to the kitchen with anyone who wanted to speak with you afterwards, while the team gently, and almost imperceptibly, guides everyone to the door.

JO'S STORY:

Mid-April: The committee did not stop their work while their fundraising applications were being considered, but instead carried on. They wanted to introduce the Family Dining Project to the community that they hoped would both support and benefit from it. They booked the venue that they were planning to hire as their base for the delivery of their service, for a weekday evening, at 6.30 p.m. six weeks hence. They advertised it widely, and asked their community partners to do the same. Twelve families were represented at the meeting, which the committee felt was a good beginning. Jo's presentation to these families is in Appendix C, and includes those aspects of the Project that the committee were looking for help or information on: how suitable the venue was in terms of travel for families in and around Trulegate; whether a twice-weekly meal would be welcomed; whether dining communally would be preferred to takeaway meals; whether the families knew of any other similar provision locally; if any regular events for families or for children already ran on either of the two early evenings that the Project was planned to run; what time the meals service should ideally begin; and if anyone knew of allotment-holders and independent grocers in the area that might consider donating surplus food to the Project. Jo also appealed for volunteers.

The venue was judged by the families to be easily accessible on foot, so that few families would need to find money for bus fares to get there. It had a good reputation locally, and many of the families had attended events there over the years. Some of the parents offered to volunteer – even though the Safeguarding lead pointed out that their own children would then need to be supervised by a friend or relative present at the meal, as no unsupervised children could attend because of Safeguarding concerns. All knew of several other local families who could certainly benefit, and agreed that the communal nature of the meals made it more of a social event to look forward to. Two people with allotments locally offered seasonal produce, and one additionally offered to provide flowers for the tables in the spring and summer: both were gratefully accepted. There was a suggestion from one of the allotment holders that the families might like to visit the allotment when vegetables were ready to eat, to see them harvested and then to eat the subsequent food, perhaps after a child-friendly cookery lesson. This was well-received by the participants and the committee members, and it was arranged that the person who suggested it would speak further with the committee members about this.

Someone called Bob asked whether the lonely older people on the estate could also be included in the meals, and suggested that some of these would be too physically frail to make their own way and would need free transport provided for them – perhaps volunteers picking them up in their own cars. Jo reminded Bob of the purpose of the Project, and was supported by a committee member who pointed out that there were two lunch clubs for older people running from the venue every week.

Most people took leaflets outlining the Project to give to their friends and relatives locally, and promised to sign up to – and spread the word about – the Project's Facebook page. One person, having no access to the internet at home, asked to be kept up-to-date via text. The Communications Lead was happy to agree. Everyone who was interested also gave the Communications Lead their name and mobile phone number.

ENDNOTES

1. 'How to Design & Teach Workshops that work every time. The Workshop Survival Guide'. Rob Fitzpatrick & Devin Hunt (2019).

9

POLICIES AND INSURANCE

As a committee, you will need to prepare a small number of appropriate policies that everyone adheres to, and find insurance cover relevant to your Project. Between them, these are necessary to protect the physical and emotional wellbeing of everyone involved, and your Project's assets. As a team, you will need to prepare policies on Health and Safety, Safeguarding Children and Vulnerable Adults, and on Data Protection. These will need to be tailored to: the service that your Project will be providing; how that service will be delivered; who to; where; and who by. You should also draft a policy on Volunteering, and one for the guidance of your Communications Lead related to information about, and photographs of, your service users and volunteers in publicity and fundraising. This is where the committee's additional five lead roles (mentioned in chapter 3) come to the fore, as each lead will be applying, monitoring, updating and feeding back to the committee on any and all aspects of the policy that is relevant to their area. I'll look at what to include in an Environmental Policy too, as you may well want to ensure that you're doing what you can to reduce any negative impact by your Project on the area (serendipitously, this is also increasingly looked for by funders). Below are just some outlines, and pointers to other avenues of information for you. Your local CVS should be able to provide some guidance on writing your policies too, and your partner organisations may provide advice, and could show you their respective policies as a guide. I've also cited the relevant government documents and resources for each of the main policies here. Regarding insurance, the Charity Commission has produced some guidance to help trustees decide what types of cover will be appropriate for their charity[1].

Health and Safety: your 'duty of care'

You can't just hand volunteers a wrench and say 'Yes, that boiler's a stinker. Just bash it and duck'. (Ah, the 1970s!) Health and Safety legislation is about putting sensible and proportionate controls in place to protect people from harm. As long as your Project doesn't have any employees there would only be limited circumstances when Health and Safety law would apply to yourselves, for example when volunteers are in charge of premises such as a community hall[2]. But even if Health and Safety law does not apply to your group, you will still have a 'duty of care' to each other, and to others who may be affected by your Project's activities. And individuals could sue for damages using civil law if they are injured as a result of the negligence of someone involved in your Project. So, it is more than 'doing the right thing' to agree as a committee how you can best provide and maintain a safe, clean environment for any volunteers and service users – one that is not detrimental to anyone's physical health or wellbeing, and which minimises the risk of accidents, and has sensible fire safety precautions. (The local Fire Service will be pleased to advise you on fire safety too.) Highlight too within the policy that you will provide a comprehensive induction for all your volunteers, to ensure that they and everyone else remains safe while volunteering with your Project.

There is guidance on both what your Health and Safety Policy should include, and carrying out risk assessments, on the UK Government's Health and Safety Executive (HSE) website[2 & 3], as well as examples and a template for you to adapt to your particular service provision. You'll quickly recognise that it's all just common sense really. Your Health and Safety Policy should provide your committee's Health and Safety Lead, who will be working closely with the Volunteering Lead, with a structure to ensure that the practical day-to-day working of your Project is carried out safely. In relation to protecting volunteers, it should ensure that:

- The Health and Safety Lead knows in advance how and where the volunteers are going to be utilised for any activity

- The volunteers are covered by your group's insurance policy: you should provide the same level of protection to volunteers as you would for employees

- The volunteers have the information and training that they would need to carry out the activities safely

- Effective supervision and monitoring arrangements are in place

- Accidents and near misses involving volunteers are recorded and followed up; this is all part of learning and adapting.

The committee's decisions on the content of your group's Health and Safety policy will be recorded in your meeting notes for yourselves of course, but it's also something that you'll want to write down as a summary for display on your noticeboard, and perhaps on your Facebook page with your other policies, to make everyone involved in your Project aware of it. Your lead person for Health and Safety should take new volunteers through the policy, and make sure that they understand it. And good Health and Safety procedures should be a two-way process, allowing volunteers and service users to raise concerns and influence decisions on managing health and safety.

Safeguarding

'Safeguarding' is specifically about protecting children (i.e. anyone under the age of eighteen) and *vulnerable* adults, from neglect, abuse and exploitation. I'll expand on the word 'vulnerable' later in this section. The Charity Commission places a responsibility on all of an organisation's trustees to ensure good safeguarding practice, and it is part of the wider 'Duty of Care' which stipulates that all trustees must take all reasonable steps to prevent harm to people who come into contact with their services. But, more fundamentally, you should want to prepare this policy diligently, adhere to it scrupulously and maintain it as a 'working document' which will be revised and updated as learning dictates, because protecting the vulnerable is everyone's responsibility. A member of your committee will need to take the lead on safeguarding, monitoring the application of your group's Safeguarding Policy in the day-to-day running of the Project. The Safeguarding Lead will also need to attend relevant training: apart from anything else, they need to be familiar with the signs of neglect, abuse and exploitation, and to be able to communicate that to all frontline volunteers.

The Local Authority is accountable for safeguarding in their area, having statutory responsibility for this, but that doesn't exclude any individual or group from responsibility to help protect the vulnerable, or from exercising a duty of care – it just provides a mechanism by which safeguarding is maximised as efficiently as possible. There are different structures to support adults (through Safeguarding Boards) and children (through Partnerships). Both have three core members: the Local Authority, Clinical Commissioning Groups (CCGs), and the Police. The website for your local Safeguarding Board or Partnership will include the contact details that you would need to report a concern, along with their strategic plan and annual report, which your Safeguarding Lead should read.

There is a fundamental difference in the way that children and vulnerable adults are safeguarded, and it's about whether or not you would need consent to report concerns. For children and young people under the age of eighteen, you do *not* need consent from either the child or young person themselves, or from anyone else, to report a concern: you would just contact the Local Authority's Designated Officer if you believe that a child or young person may be at risk, or has been harmed. It's much more complicated for adults: it does not include all adults, but only those deemed 'vulnerable' and who also lack capacity to make their own decisions.

An adult *could* be 'vulnerable' because of a number of factors related to their care and support needs, including, but not limited to, (advanced) age, a disability or sensory impairment, or mental ill-health. But the vast majority of adults with care and support needs have the *capacity* to make their own decisions, and that includes the right to make foolish decisions, just like everyone else. How many times have you looked back at an incident and thought 'Why did I....?' 'What made me think I should...?' In the same way, if someone makes a decision that you think is not in their best interests, that's not necessarily about their *capacity*. It could be about personal choice. So, as long as a vulnerable adult has capacity, their consent would be needed before the Local Authority could intervene – unless there are specific circumstances involving for example a child or criminal behaviour, or imminent danger of serious harm or death. If it's not something that requires a 999 call to the emergency services, and if you are in any doubt about whether a concern you have could be reported, contact the Safeguarding Board in your area to ask them.

It's worth noting too that under the Data Protection Act (2018), which we'll be looking at in the next section of this chapter, there are very specific circumstances in which you would be able to give someone's personal details out without their permission –

i.e. only when 'this would be crucial to prevent serious harm or distress or where someone's life is threatened'[4]. And in any other circumstances, without the permission of the adult involved, the Local Authority is unlikely to decide that it is a safeguarding issue.

Your Safeguarding Policy should set out your Project's overall approach to safeguarding: *how* you will carry it out effectively (i.e. your 'procedures'), and *why* (i.e. the key principles underlying the policy).

Your **procedures** would include your committee's safeguarding priorities, and plans for improvement through monitoring and learning from the Project's activities. They would spell out what you are responsible for as a Project in terms of safeguarding, and how you will train and support the team so that they will recognise, respond to, report, record and refer safeguarding concerns appropriately. You will be highlighting the Safeguarding Lead as the key contact, and explaining the process should that person be unreachable. Everyone needs to know that concerns could be reported directly to the relevant Safeguarding Board or Partnership if the Safeguarding Lead is unavailable – and you should ensure that the contact details for both organisations are clearly displayed. The person reporting their concerns directly does need to understand that the Safeguarding Lead or at least a member of the committee must be informed of the issue and of steps taken as soon as practicable, as the Project's representatives will have procedures to carry out in relation to the safeguarding concern – from recording the incident(s) to taking appropriate steps to exclude the individual against whom an allegation has been made.

Your policy's key **principles** should include the six principles of safeguarding embedded in the Care Act (2014), and outlined on the SCIE website[5]:

- **Empowerment** – this is really about facilitating informed consent

- **Prevention** – as it's always better to take action before any harm occurs

- **Proportionality** – the least intrusive response appropriate to the risk presented

- **Protection** – support and representation for those in greatest need

- **Partnerships** – local services working with their communities, all of whom have a part to play in preventing, detecting, and reporting neglect and abuse

- **Accountability** and transparency in safeguarding practise.

Your Safeguarding Policy needs to be tailored to your specific service and to the people utilising that service – it might involve, for example, stipulating that children will be accompanied by their parents or carers at all times while utilising your service. Fundamentally, it needs to help to protect service users from abuse and exploitation. And this policy will also ensure that your committee members and volunteers, and indeed other service users, will be protected from false allegations of abuse or exploitation – because they should never be in a situation where they are vulnerable to these allegations, e.g. alone with a child. Any accusations would need to be reported to the Police: think about how it would feel to be a falsely accused person, and the impact that it would have personally and professionally. Build in measures to make sure that it doesn't happen.

Speak with your local CVS for guidance on drafting your Safeguarding Policy, and probably for training opportunities. And there are extensive guidelines on safeguarding children on the Government's designated website[6]. Training is provided by the NSPCC, and there is guidance on their website for keeping children safe in voluntary and community organisations. For the appropriate safeguarding of vulnerable adults, the 'Social Care Institute of Excellence' (SCIE)[7] provides training, and their website is very useful too. And NCVO's website has a guide to preparing Safeguarding policies[8].

Data Protection Policy

General Data Protection Regulation (GDPR) came into force on 1st January 2021, though the preparations began in the Third Sector a couple of years before that date (the prospect of eye-wateringly high fines for breaches focused everyone's attention!). It is underpinned by the UK Government's Data Protection Act (2018), and basically it's a set of rules about collecting and storing personal information on people. I'll outline this as it applies to most small organisations (i.e. those with an income of under £100,000* per year)[9].

Firstly, I'll mention the iCO (information Commissioner's Office). This is an independent authority for the UK, 'set up to uphold information rights in the public interest, promoting openness by public bodies and data privacy for individuals'[10]. The iCO have a website and a helpline, and they will help your Data Protection lead and your committee to ensure that every aspect of gathering, disseminating, storing and destroying information is carried out appropriately. Registration with iCO would almost certainly be free for you, whether your group has charity status or becomes a CIC or CLG. This is because organisations processing limited personal information solely for not-for-profit purposes are exempt from the current £40 annual fee (2022 prices). You don't have to register with iCO if you are exempt from paying their annual fee (there's a 'self-assessment fee checker' on their website to find out). But even if you don't have to register, why not join anyway? It's a useful organisation, and a good resource for your Data Protection lead – you will still need to comply with your data protection obligations, and the staff at the iCO could help with that.

There are certain key words that you must keep in mind when you are gathering information (or 'data'). It needs to be:

- **Relevant** and **necessary** to the purpose of collecting it, e.g. If you want to find out about dietary requirements, you wouldn't need to ask what area someone lives in. But if you were asking about transport links to the Project then that information becomes both relevant and necessary

- **Processed securely** – only accessible by one or two strictly relevant people, and held safely, in a password-protected computer file, or a locked box in a secure office

- It needs to have a **'lawful basis'**. There are six lawful bases, but the best one for our purposes is **'consent'**. The individual providing you with their personal information will have given their informed consent, allowing you to process their relevant personal data for a specific purpose that has been explained to them. Consent 'means offering individuals real choice and control. Genuine consent should put individuals in charge, build trust and engagement, and enhance your reputation.'[10]. Consent must specifically cover: the Project's name, the reason you're collecting this information, how you'll process the information, and what you'll do with it afterwards

- **Destroyed** – after it is no longer necessary for the purpose for which it was gathered, deleting the electronic file and any back-ups, and removing it from the 'recycle bin' of the computer system – and if you've sent the information within emails they need to be deleted from your 'sent' folder and the recipients' 'in box' too. Use a cross shredder for paper copies.

The **'Privacy Notice'** – as a small organisation, you won't need to specifically 'document' or keep a record of your occasional information-gathering work – i.e. what personal data you hold, where it came from, what you do with it and why you hold it, and who you share it with – though you might want to. You are just required to explain the *purpose* of your data-gathering in a clear and concise Privacy Notice that you'll be sharing with everyone just before they give you their personal information. Every Privacy Notice is specific to each piece of research, but *all* should include:

- Your Project's contact details

- The types of personal data you'll be collecting

- Why you have collected this information and what you're going to do with it

- Your lawful basis, i.e. consent. Be careful how you phrase that, so that people don't think that they're legally obliged to tell you

- Who you will share this information with

- How long you'll hold it before disposing of it securely

- The fact that they can refuse consent, or withdraw consent (and have their information deleted) after they've given it – and tell them how to do this. And emphasise that consent is not a precondition for accessing your service

- Details of how they can complain if they've got concerns about the way you're using their information.

For example: [Project name] is collecting information to find out food preferences among local older people. This information will be used to ensure that people who come to the Friday lunch club can all enjoy a suitable meal option. Within three weeks of gathering all this information, we will understand which meals or ingredients are to be avoided, and the information provided by each individual will then be destroyed. We need your 'informed consent' before we ask you any questions, but you are under absolutely no obligation to provide this information, and it certainly won't affect your access to the Project's services in any way if you decide not to take part. If you do choose to provide this information for us, it will only be seen by the committee's Data Protection lead and up to two other specific committee members involved in collecting and collating this information, and it will be held in a locked box in a secure room (and / or on a password-protected computer file) until it is destroyed. If you decide that you want to withdraw your information, you can tell us that at any time (contact details below) and we will destroy it. Just phone us on: [................] or email us at [................]. And if you have any questions, comments, concerns, or indeed complaints, please contact us using this same phone number / email address.

There is guidance on writing your Privacy Notice, and a template, on the iCO's website.

Even if you're just planning to ask for and record someone's contact details, you would need to be able to: justify why you need that; explain that justification to the service user; assure them that it will be stored securely and deleted after a predetermined length of time, e.g. a month after they stop attending the Project. There is even stronger legal protection for more sensitive information, such as ethnic background, religious beliefs and health, and separate safeguards for personal data relating to criminal convictions and offences. Contact the iCO for guidance if any of the information that you need to gather could be considered sensitive.

The committee member leading on Data Protection should monitor the Project's compliance with Data Protection policies. That person should also keep evidence of consent: who, when, how and what was told to people. And, as with all committee members with additional responsibilities, they should keep the rest of the committee informed of any problems, along with steps taken or needed to resolve this etc.

As an aside: you'll come across some terminology on the iCO website that differentiates between two types of information collectors – i.e. 'controllers' and 'processors'. For our purposes you're a 'controller', as you make the decisions as to what data to gather and process, and what it will be used for. ('Processors' are third parties acting on instructions from controllers.)

Volunteering

Your Volunteering Policy is where you would set out what volunteers should expect from you and what you will expect from them, and what happens if your expectations aren't met. You need to have decided as a committee what this Policy will include / stipulate – you don't really want to be 'making it up as you go along', which will lead to inconsistency and to the perception that some volunteers are being treated differently to others. It provides a useful structure for induction, training, supervision and monitoring, and – in case it becomes necessary – for disciplinary procedures and dismissal. If you have standard guidance then everyone knows the score, and your committee members and lead volunteers will have appropriate 'back-up' for their legitimate actions. The chapter following this one, on recruiting, supervising and retaining volunteers, will give you a sense of what a Volunteering Policy should include, and your local CVS should help you further.

Utilising information or photographs of your Service Users or Volunteers in Publicity or Fundraising

As mentioned in chapter 3, you'll want a Communications Lead from your committee. Their role would include updating and monitoring your Facebook page, and providing content for the media, for articles in newsletters etc. Any information used, e.g. perhaps in the form of case studies, would need the permission and involvement of the person concerned. It should not include that person's last name, nor where they live. For example, if you're referring to a vulnerable older person living alone, you really don't want criminals to be able to find out where they are to be found – and you'll all have seen articles where this stipulation wasn't given to journalists – e.g. 'Mabel Bloggs of Short Road is so pleased to have joined the Faux Area Gateaux and Gossip group, as before joining the group she says that she hadn't spoken to anyone in four months…' Taking and publishing photos would need the written permission of each subject, and for those under the age of eighteen that permission will need to be from a parent or guardian. You would of course tell people what you would be using the information or photos for. Don't take photographs too often, and don't allow anyone outside your Project to take photos: it's disruptive and potentially intrusive. (Any media interviews should be by prior arrangement, and under the guidance of the Communications Lead.)

Environmental Policy

Your organisation is not required to have an Environmental Policy, though those registered with Companies House have an 'environmental duty' to take into account 'the impact of the company's operations on … the environment'[11]. But it's no bad thing to ensure that the impact of your Project on the environment will be as close to zero as possible, and to demonstrate your commitment to that. And funders are increasingly keen to learn that you have an Environmental Policy, even if they don't ask to see it. Charity Excellence Framework (CEF)[12] has produced some invaluable (free to utilise) guidance on writing this, and has a template that you could download. And the 'Waste Hierarchy' that they outline is a very straightforward tool to guide your thinking when you begin to draft the Policy:

1. **Eliminate** – avoid producing waste in the first place

2. **Reduce** – minimise the amount of waste you do produce

3. **Re-Use** – use items as many times as possible

4. **Recycle** – recycle what you can only after you have re-used it

5. **Dispose** – dispose of what's left in a responsible way.

There is no set format for an Environmental Policy, but I'd suggest that you start with a brief outline of the activities of your Project. Then think about the environmental impact of these activities – positives such as utilising surplus food or re-using school uniforms, and negatives such as the impact of transporting goods – and how you could implement any practical and realistic changes. Then you might want to use the five sections outlined below[2] as a framework for the main body of the policy, relating each section to your specific Project, with accompanying achievable objectives:

Materials and Resources. This covers everything from buying stationery in bulk – which reduces the impact of transporting goods on the environment (and saves money) – to replacing plastic bottles at your meetings with water jugs and glasses.

Managing Waste. You'll no doubt already be recycling cardboard, glass, paper and plastics. You could also recycle mobile phones and printer cartridges (which could give you some income), use environmentally friendly cleaning products etc. You can apply for free waste disposal help from the Hippo 'Grants up for Grabs scheme'[3].

Energy Use. Here you'll just be applying what you already do at home to the venue that your Project will run from: turning off lights in empty rooms, switching off electrical equipment when it's not in use etc. There is guidance provided by the Carbon Trust on saving energy[4].

Water Use. The suggestions on the CEF website include keeping a jug of water in the fridge so that you're not running the water in the tap until it's cold, and organising the repair of dripping taps. Think about water use within your particular Project and at your fundraising events etc.

Emissions and Transport. Suggestions here include arranging meetings at a location that minimises travel for people – if it's not possible to meet online.

The objectives that you stipulate in these five sections would form the basis of an accompanying Action Plan, which will set targets and timescales for your objectives. For example, if one of your objectives is to use recycled stationery to reduce CO_2 emissions and save trees, a target could be 'identifying a low-cost supplier of recycled paper' and the deadline 'within the next month'. A further target for the same objective could be to 'use 100% recycled paper' and the target 'within three months of identifying an appropriate supplier'. And if you secure sufficient funding for the laptops and smartphones that your Project may need, your target might ultimately be a paperless office.

Resources for practical advice include:

Every Action Counts[15] – 'provides free access to information, action planning tools, publications and trained Community Champions', to enable you to reduce the impact of your Project on the environment and care for your local area.

Carbon Trust[14] – works with organisations to reduce their environmental impact. The Carbon Trust has produced free 'Office Energy Efficiency' guides that you could access and download.

City Bridge Trust[16] – if your Project is in Greater London, you could apply for a free eco-audit from City Bridge Trust.

Insurance:

You'll need to take out some insurance to protect the Project and everyone either involved in it or affected by its services – your volunteers and service users, your equipment, your income sources, members of the public attending your fundraising activities etc. The Charity Commission has produced some guidance to help trustees to decide what insurance will be appropriate for their charity[1], and recommends utilising an insurance broker who has an understanding of charities' insurance needs; NCVO could recommend one. Buying insurance is one way in which trustees can properly protect their assets and resources, and you may need:

- Buildings insurance

- Contents insurance

- Event insurance – e.g. if you're running a fete to raise funds, you may want to insure against loss of earnings in the event of poor weather leading to a disappointing turn out

- For insurance purposes, charities are advised to treat volunteers in the same way as employees are treated, and to ensure that they are covered by insurance such as Employers' Liability or Public Liability cover

- Public liability cover may be appropriate for charities too who own or occupy land or buildings, and also for charities that carry on a business activity away from their own premises or arrange events attended by the public. Public liability cover insures against claims from third parties** for bodily injury / illness, or loss or damage to property inflicted in the course of the activity or event. (Make sure that it covers legal costs too [12])

- The Charities Act (2011) also allows trustees to buy trustee indemnity insurance and pay the premiums out of their charity's funds

- Organisations that own or operate motor vehicles are required by law to buy motor insurance, providing cover against third party injury and property damage.

This is not a complete list, of course. Other potential areas for cover listed in the document referenced (1) include insurance against theft by anyone involved in the Project, for example. All potential insurance needs are worth exploring with your broker if they are appropriate for your Project.

It's worth noting here that volunteers do need to notify their insurance company if they are using their own vehicle to transport passengers or goods for you. The vast majority of insurance companies will not increase a volunteer's premiums for this, but if a volunteer has an accident in their car whilst volunteering for you, and hasn't notified their insurance company of their role, then they will probably not be covered by their insurance policy. RoSPA has produced a Volunteer Drivers' Handbook[17] which includes the law as it relates to driving as a volunteer.

Further Reading:

https://assets.publishing.service.gov.uk/government/uploads/system/uploads/attachment_data/fil e/284703/rs17text.pdf

Going Green: Charities and Environmental Responsibility (N.B. some of their links / information about resources are out of date now.)

ENDNOTES

*N.B. Organisations with an income between £100,000 and £1 million are considered medium-sized [9].

** 'Third parties – someone who is not one of the two main people [or entities] involved in a legal agreement but is still affected in some way [18.]

1. https://www.gov.uk/government/publications/charities-and-insurance-cc49/charities-and-insurance

2. https://www.hse.gov.uk/legislation/

3. Volunteering: How to manage the risks. hse.gov.uk/voluntary/index.htm

4. scie.org.uk/safeguarding/adults/practice/questions – Social Care Institute of Excellence

5. scie.org.uk/safeguarding/ulo/trustees/guide#duty-of-care

6. www.gov.uk/topic/schools-colleges-childrens-services/safeguarding-children

7. SCIE – https://www.scie.org.uk/

8. https://www.ncvo.org.uk/help-and-guidance/safeguarding/steps-safer-organisation/policies -and-procedures/#

9. NCVO's UK Civil Society Almanac 2021 https://www.ncvo.org.uk/news-and-insights/news-index/uk-civil-society-almanac-2021/#/

10. ico.org.uk

11. Companies Act 2006 – Section 172 (1) (d) – 'A director of a company must …have regard (amongst other matters) to…. the impact of the company's operations on the community and the environment.'

12. Charity Excellence Framework's guidance on preparing an Environmental Policy: https://www.charityexcellence.co.uk/Home/BlogDetail?Link=Charity_Environmental_Policy _Template

13. https://www.hippowaste.co.uk/charity-community/

14. www.carbontrust.co.uk

15. www.everyactioncounts.org.uk

16. https://www.citybridgetrust.org.uk/what-we-do/grant-making/what-we-fund/connecting-t he-capital/eco-audits/

17. https://www.rospa.com/road-safety/resources/free cited by CEF

18. Britannia.com

10

RECRUITING AND
RETAINING VOLUNTEERS

N o doubt you will need volunteers for your Project, and this
chapter is about how to find them, and how best to keep them
engaged and motivated to regularly support your Project. You
might be wondering why you would need this though – after all, you'll
probably begin with a few people who you know, either directly or
indirectly, and they will be content to just pitch in and do what needs
to be done. But if your Project relies exclusively on the same volunteers day in and day out, doing the same tasks, they will gradually fall
away, most likely from flagging motivation or exhaustion. Quite aside
from the fact that it's not fair to ask this of anyone, you don't want to
lose good volunteers. This would leave you short-handed, reduce
the scope of your service, lessen the pool of fresh ideas and insights
that volunteers could provide, mean that you have to spend valuable
time and resources recruiting, inducting, training and supervising new
volunteers, and impact negatively on any plans you might have to expand your service. Sustainability relies to an extent on the appropriate
turnover of motivated and well supported volunteers and, especially
for those volunteers who may be with you for the longer term, to
their movement within the Project to roles with different challenges,
requiring different skills. The points noted here should, in the long

run, save you time and frustration, and help to ensure that volunteer retention is high, and that your Project flourishes.

Finding volunteers

Firstly you will need to understand exactly what each of your volunteering roles will involve. Summarise every role separately in a few lines, explaining how service users will be benefiting from your Project, and highlighting the tasks involved in the role, any skills needed, and the benefits to the volunteer (in addition to satisfying their altruism). Open with an attention-grabbing headline, followed by how they could make a difference. For example, 'There are 10,000 lonely older people in your city. You can change that – help get the party started.' Then, depending on the make-up of the community in your local area – for example, whether it's predominantly older retired people, young parents, people looking for work etc. – you'd emphasise different aspects of the volunteering role, from the social aspects of the volunteering team, to the opportunities to develop and build upon their skills.

- Word of mouth is the 'gold standard' recruiter, so hopefully volunteers will want to bring in their circle of friends, relations and colleagues too

- Your local CVS will probably run a volunteering brokerage service, and there may be a separate Volunteer Bureau too for your area

- Your local council may advertise volunteering roles

- Your group's Facebook page could feature your need for volunteers

- You could revisit the links you've built with other media outlets through the work that you did to promote the event with the local community (chapter 8)

- Volunteers *may* be recruited from local faith groups – though these might already be heavily committed with the initiatives already running from their place of worship

- Social / hobby groups in the area might be useful too, if their interests align with your Project's volunteering roles – e.g. allotment association members if you're going to be using fresh produce, cycling clubs if you'll be delivering by bike...

- Your local schools may feature your need for volunteers in their newsletter for parents

- A local university may be interested in promoting your need for volunteers to students (just bear in mind rota-wise that you'll get most students term-time only, and outside exam revision weeks)

- There are 'Employability Services' in many areas, either run directly by the Department for Work and Pensions (DWP), the local council, or by a private company. These often recognise that well-supported volunteering roles are a useful way to gain many of the skills needed in the workplace. Just search for 'Employability Services in [town/city]', and / or ask at your local Job Centre

- And there's a UK charity called 'Media Trust'[1] which matches volunteers who have media know-how to groups such as yours; they could support you in your work to recruit volunteers (and in raising the profile of your Project).

You'll notice that I didn't suggest contacting the local groups and organisations that you have a relationship with, to ask for help with volunteer recruitment: they will be very protective of their own service's volunteers. That's just the way it is.

Think about who's going to supervise your Project's volunteers.

Ask yourself who among your committee has the skills and time to support and manage their fellow volunteers well. Volunteers will demonstrate great commitment and work tirelessly to fulfil the aims of the Project, but require more effort to recruit and retain than paid staff, and more on-going support, as well as induction, training opportunities, supervision and monitoring, regular well-earned praise and recognition, and someone to feed back to them all the positives that result from their work as part of the team. And, even at the outset of your Project, your Volunteering Lead will need to identify the first one or two 'co-ordinators' among the volunteers – people who will organise rotas, make sure supplies get collected or distributed, ensure that significant events in volunteers' lives are flagged for acknowledgement etc.

How many volunteers will you need?

Think about how many volunteers you'll need, realistically. You need to strike a balance between having volunteers standing idle and frustrated at their time being wasted, and being over-reliant on a handful of committed volunteers working until they're on their knees. It's awful for volunteers to feel under pressure to turn up – it's not supposed to be a chore, and they won't stay.

To decide how many volunteers you'll need, just ask yourself:

- What needs to be done?

- How long will these tasks take?

- How often will they need to be carried out?

- How much time is available within the team for volunteers' supervision and support?

The committee member taking the lead on all things volunteer-related will need to be aware of the number of hours that each volunteer would be available each week, and what times and days each would be available to volunteer with the Project. Think of it as a work schedule – e.g. one volunteer is needed for two hours every afternoon, and three volunteers are needed every other Friday lunchtime etc. And, like a work schedule, you need to build in holiday / sickness cover etc. alongside the traditional drops in volunteer numbers – e.g. school holidays for parents of younger children, and students travelling home after their summer term ends. Retired volunteers will be particularly helpful here, though they'll probably want to go on holiday too! If possible, have a pool of 'reserve' volunteers ready to step in at short notice.

Volunteer roles

The volunteering roles on offer within your Project won't appeal to everyone – that's just not possible. But their appeal or otherwise is something that potential volunteers should find out before any time is invested by your committee. This begins with well-defined volunteering roles. If volunteers have misunderstood what the role is, and believe they are signing up for something else entirely, or are still unsure or confused as to their role after they arrive, they are unlikely to stay.

For example: the first volunteering I did was as a sixteen year old, in a long-stay provision for people with severe learning disabilities and physical disabilities. It was a hectic environment. The frontline staff were genuinely far too busy to manage, direct, support and supervise the young volunteers that arrived on a Wednesday from the local school. And no-one within the provision had taken responsibility for ensuring that volunteers had appropriate tasks to carry out, safely, to support the people living there. So when I arrived, someone literally just waved her hand vaguely around and said 'Oh, you know. Go and help out.' We all became an added chore for staff, rather than a potentially valuable resource, and no volunteer returned more than once.

Potential volunteers should know upfront what will be expected of them, and will want to understand the positive difference that they will make to your service users.

Draft 'Job Descriptions' for each volunteering role

Job descriptions allow you to gauge whether each role is properly defined and whether it has enough of the 'good stuff' to keep a volunteer committed and engaged, i.e. interesting, challenging, leading to upskilling, providing training opportunities, utilising their existing skills etc. You'll also utilise the job description to spell out the volunteers' duties in terms of your expectations of them and their behaviour while they are representing your Project: illustrate what words like 'discretion' and 'respect' mean within that volunteering role at your Project – how they should be applied on a daily basis – as well as 'politeness' and the more prosaic 'reliability' etc. And if any role includes a disproportionate number of the least popular tasks, a detailed job description will enable you to recognise this and be able to share them out across the volunteering roles; volunteering is supposed to be enjoyable!

A job description allows a potential volunteer to see at a glance if a particular role is for them: before you've spent time and money processing the relevant paperwork, and inducting and training them. And it allows you to show them the personal benefits of the role – for example, the way in which the role provides upskilling, training and experience that will be transferable to the job market. It's one of the ways of attracting volunteers, and retaining them. For example, the experience volunteers gain in person-centred skills will be transferable to absolutely any job. Stipulate the minimum time commitment you'd expect from a volunteer, and explain why this is. (It's likely to be because of the time and resources needed to induct them etc., and possibly because the service users that are being supported need stability.) Stress the timings of the Project's services – it's quite frustrating to spend time and other resources on a potential volunteer only to find they're only available for five minutes every third Tuesday. You should also stipulate prominently within the job description whether you will be paying volunteers' expenses. And, if so, will it be just travel, or subsistence too? (Don't exclude local volunteers who might only be able to join you if their bus fares are paid, for example: you just need to build this expense into funding bids.) You should review your job descriptions annually, in partnership with your existing volunteers.

The first steps to making potential volunteers valued members of the team

- **Tell them what happens next.** Your potential volunteers will have read the job description and have decided that they'd like to find out more. Outline the process that they'll need to undergo before they can volunteer without direct supervision within your Project: everything from identity checks to induction and a relatively informal period of supervision. Because, while aspects of the job description may be negotiable, the induction and supervision process is not. Explain the reasons for each stage. If they're committed, all will be well. If they object to any aspect of it, even after your explanation of its purpose, it's best to know now. It is there to help protect your service users, your team and your Project's reputation.

- Once you've been up and running for a while, and have some volunteers experienced in their respective roles, you could **introduce subsequent newbies to experienced volunteers** within your team. This will provide new volunteers with an insight into the role that they're interested in, and give them an idea of how each role interconnects to support the Project, and where they and their chosen role fits in to the whole service: each volunteer needs to understand that they are integral to the successful delivery of your Project. Give them a chance to chat and to ask questions about the role and any aspects of the Project. While your Project is brand new though, your first volunteers are 'trail-blazers' and can help considerably in tailoring the roles to the needs of the Project's service users. I wouldn't suggest that your initial volunteers gain experience at a similar Project elsewhere. This is for two main reasons: they may pick up bad habits (e.g. thinking that it's okay to store donated food in their car overnight, because they see that done by the volunteers of another not-for-profit food provider; in fact that's an Environmental Health violation) or they may get settled there and decide to stay at that Project!

- The next step would be asking the potential volunteer to complete an '**application form**' for you. This can be very straightforward – just contact details, a brief background, a note on when they'd be available to volunteer, and details of two referees. It's best not to put this form online: it's good to speak with enquirers before they complete an application form. You'll want to find out: if they've read and understood the job description, and would be available on the day / at the time that they'd be required; if they have any literacy problems that might make it difficult for them to complete the form without support; or if they lack the tech to complete, print off or submit it. And this will give prospective volunteers the opportunity to ask some initial questions about the Project and the role too.

- **Take up references.** This may at first glance seem excessive for Projects supporting adults rather than children, but adults can be vulnerable too (both service users and volunteers), perhaps because of a learning disability, a mental health challenge, or just because they are naïve and trusting. Anyone wearing a tabard or a name badge is generally perceived to be a trustworthy person, and will be in a position to build potentially exploitative relationships with both service users and with their fellow volunteers. It is your responsibility to protect the people involved in your Project in every way that's available to you, and to protect your Project's reputation. Neither of a volunteer's two references should be provided by a family member. Decide whether you'd accept references from friends and neighbours as well as employers and work colleagues etc. Tell applicants when you'll be contacting their referees, and always do so: don't just assume that because they've supplied details of referees then you'll hear good things about the volunteer from them. *I once received a volunteer application from someone who supplied only the name of his mother and his Probation Officer as referees, and frankly neither had a good word to say about him. That sort of thing should raise some flags!*

- Then the Committee member taking the lead on managing the Project's volunteers will need to arrange a **semi-informal chat** with the prospective volunteer. However this is structured, the job description should guide the more targeted questions. Ask them in advance to bring the necessary **IDs**, as this is the time to make sure that the volunteer is who they say they are, by looking at their photo ID and something else 'official' with their home address on – maybe a utility bill or bank statement. It is necessary to check IDs because volunteers can misrepresent themselves and, if they abuse their position and provide an incorrect name and address, the consequences – over and above those experienced by the people involved in your Project – will include not being able to give the relevant authorities accurate information as to their identity and whereabouts. The Project's reputation will be severely damaged too. As with contacting referees, it's an insurance to safeguard everyone involved in the Project – you hope you'll never need it, but it's there if you do. It is better to do it, than to try to justify why you didn't carry out these simple procedures if something occurs to the detriment of your service users, your team or your Project.

This semi-informal chat is also an opportunity to discuss with the potential volunteer whether the role is within their **physical capabilities**. If it isn't, and if no reasonable adjustments would make it so, then discuss other potential volunteering roles if that's possible. This chat is also when you would find out the volunteer's motivations for volunteering with you – whether they want to make friends, experience leadership roles etc. This will help you to make each volunteer's time with you more productive for both them and the Project, and you'll retain them for much longer. And this is where you'll be able to **clarify vague statements** such as 'I'm available anytime and happy doing anything' into 'Well, I could do Tuesdays after 5 p.m. or Saturday mornings, and my social confidence is a bit rusty so a chance to work in a friendly team would be great.'[2]

• At this stage you would start the process of clearance through the **Disclosure and Barring Service (DBS)**, if that's applicable to the volunteering role. Visit the website of the UK Government's Disclosure and Barring Service (DBS) to read the guidance that will indicate if any of your volunteering roles require (or even allow for) a DBS check, either standard or enhanced. And if you're still not sure, contact the DBS direct. If any roles do require a DBS check, you'll need to identify an organisation to process and countersign these for you. To save time though, your Volunteering Lead or another committee member could check through the completed form before it is looked at by the counter-signatory. There are several common errors to look for, including: not using black ink; not recording a maiden name / date of marriage, although they call themselves 'Mrs' (and keeping a birth surname after marriage isn't that common); using Tippex; and not signing or dating the form. Your counter-signatory will check through the form thoroughly too (though you'd be paying the fine from the DBS for a form submitted without all the appropriate information). They will also verify the volunteer's identity through photo ID and e.g. utility bills. And, of course, if volunteering roles require a DBS check, and *any* members of the committee are carrying out those roles, they will need a DBS check too – there are no exceptions.

You could also ask the volunteer to tell you about anything that's going to be flagged up on the DBS report, up front. Reassure them that, for example, three points on their driving licence for speeding will not exclude them from volunteering as a driver for you (unless of course it would for your Project!) If any convictions etc. are flagged up in a DBS check that are not something serious enough to be an immediate 'no' for the committee's Volunteering Lead, they will have to inform the potential volunteer that this will be discussed discreetly with the committee's Safeguarding Lead and Chair. Do not gossip – it will impinge on data protection regulations, and it's neither kind nor good for your Project's reputation.

- **Induction** – The Volunteering Lead should set out a framework for a volunteer's induction, as would be expected for a member of paid staff: The first day and time should be pre-arranged, in consultation with the existing volunteers that the newbie will need to meet with or be introduced to. The Volunteering Lead should think about what the new volunteer needs to know, at what stage they need to know it by, who they need to speak with, be introduced to etc. And throughout the period of induction, they will need to make sure that newbies see and understand the practical application of 'discretion', 'respect' etc. for that volunteering role at your Project. The Volunteering Lead should take them through each of the Policies outlined in chapter 9. (And the Health and Safety Lead should revisit the Health and Safety Policy with volunteers – the two leads will work quite closely together.) This induction period should take place alongside the newbie's volunteering role, if all the appropriate checks have been carried out.

- **Mentoring** – Once you have a base of experienced volunteers, you might want to think about a mentor / buddying system whereby longer-serving volunteers are matched with the newbies. But not all your volunteers – however invaluable and long-serving – will be comfortable as a mentor, and some will lack the skills or confidence to guide, teach or train others. It's not something to try to coax people into. If a mentor is not able to properly support, guide and supervise the volunteer, they themselves will be off-balance, and their mentee won't be able to flourish in their chosen volunteering role. Also, ask yourself whether the person you have in mind as a mentor is a good representative for your organisation – choose wisely! For those experienced lead volunteers that are both suitable and up for it, it's another string to their bow, providing experience in supervision and leadership.

• **Supervision** – In the end, supervision is about making sure that the volunteer carries out their chosen role usefully and efficiently – because that is the purpose of the volunteers within your Project. To achieve this, the Volunteering Lead will need to provide support tailored to each individual volunteer, which is done most effectively through, and as a result of, regular one-to-one supervision meetings in a safe and private space. Your Volunteering Lead will probably want to start the monthly supervision sessions about two weeks after the volunteer begins their role – though they should make themselves available to the newbie at specific times in the interim (perhaps at those hours in the week when the Project's services run?) The first supervision session should give new volunteers the opportunity to reflect on the process and the role, and to feed that back to you, so that you can learn from that and address any issues – both for the individual, and related to the Project and the induction process itself.

Your Volunteering Lead – who will have spoken with the new volunteer's mentor before a session – may want to open the supervision sessions with any positive feedback that has been received about specific tasks or activities that the volunteer has done well[3].

During the session, your Volunteering Lead will want to learn:

• how the volunteer feels about their volunteering role: whether they're enjoying it, or feel overwhelmed, or don't understand all the aspects of it etc., or indeed whether they've identified a better way of doing something;

- whether they need additional training;

- or a longer induction;

- that they know how to use any equipment that they are operating, safely, and have been given enough guidance to carry out all their tasks successfully;

- how comfortable and accepted they feel within the wider volunteering team;

- how valued they feel by the organisation as a whole;

- what's going on in their lives – but only if they want to share that. This isn't nosiness (or it certainly shouldn't be!), but rather a way of finding out whether anything going on in the volunteer's life will impact on their volunteering role. Don't press. And if something does come up, for example, if someone tells the Volunteering Lead that they are afraid of their abusive partner, do not give advice (see later in this chapter). The Lead can offer a listening ear and discretion, and could signpost the volunteer to sources of help. But, as you'll recall from the Safeguarding section of chapter nine, the Lead won't be able to report any concerns without the consent of the person involved (unless under the specific circumstances outlined in the section on Safeguarding);

- about any relatively minor concerns such as turning up late once or perhaps twice: be specific, giving dates and times, and an outline of the incident, behaviour or action and the consequences of that within the Project. This provides the opportunity to address issues before they escalate[3];

- whether volunteers are claiming their expenses (if they want to do so);

- about any concerns they might have about Health and Safety or Safeguarding – though volunteers should understand the procedure and timescale for reporting both as they arise, through the induction process that they will have undergone.

Over time, the sessions will of course change in nature, becoming more about getting feedback from volunteers and perhaps supporting them in their mentoring role etc. On-going support is necessary for the morale and retention of all your volunteers, however long they have been with you – it's not just for the newbies. The Volunteering Lead should keep records of the supervision sessions, accessible only to them and the volunteer, and – if a situation arises where it becomes necessary – the Chair, Health and Safety Lead or Safeguarding Lead. Keep any notes in a locked box in a secure room, or on a password-protected computer file.

Recognition

Make sure that the volunteers understand the importance of them to the Project. Keep note of volunteer hours and maybe issue certificates, badges etc. at certain markers. This shouldn't be perceived as a 'tokenistic' gesture – your volunteers are truly invaluable, and this should be a way to show that you genuinely treasure them. Have a volunteer get-together a couple of times a year (you could build this in to funding applications). You could, for example, combine a day of training and an awards presentation with a social evening, or just spend a day having a laugh together over a meal and / or an activity that everyone would enjoy – whatever works for the team.

If your volunteers feel nurtured and valued they'll stay with you, which saves you more on recruiting, inducting, training etc., but also it's just the right thing to do! Periodic get-togethers, and some small acknowledgement of volunteers' birthdays etc. makes for a happy team, and a better atmosphere for service users. Volunteers will build lasting friendships which will be of benefit to their emotional wellbeing, and that will also ensure a strong and mutually supportive volunteering team.

WhatsApp

Having an official WhatsApp group can be a useful communication tool, though people within the group will need to understand and accept that their mobile phone number will be displayed for every participant to see. Your volunteers could easily communicate with each other and you about important things such as travel delays, sickness and so on in a fast and effective way. It can also be a positive means for volunteers to share useful bits of local information or links to interesting or helpful articles that might have an impact on your Project. However, WhatsApp groups can become a hot-bed of gossip which might be hurtful or damaging, or even lead to GDPR breaches; your Communications Lead would need to be actively involved in monitoring input for the official WhatsApp group. Your volunteers may set up their own group to chat outside of their volunteering hours, and you'd need to make it clear that your volunteers are still bound by the confidentiality implicit in their roles even when outside the Project and outside the official WhatsApp group.

Monitoring and Evaluation of volunteers

The monitoring and evaluation of volunteers will be part of your Project-wide M&E (later, in chapter 12). This aspect of it would be the responsibility of your Volunteering Lead, and is crucial to the organisation's learning and continued growth, and also to nip any discontent in the bud. Additionally you might spot skills among your volunteering team that could be nurtured and utilised further. Ask volunteers what they are enjoying / how they are gaining from their time with you, what they don't like etc. This will enable you to tweak roles and reflect that in future job descriptions. Monitoring and evaluation has other benefits too in terms of volunteers' contentment and growth: people will feel valued, and recognise that their opinion matters if you're making time for a one to one (where you can't be overhead), and they see a positive outcome to their comments. And the invaluable feedback from volunteers will help to keep your Project relevant to the Community that you serve, and could lead to innovative new volunteering roles being created.

The Disciplinary and Dismissal process

I'll just begin with some reassurance: it is very rare indeed that you would need to dismiss volunteers. The more likely scenario is that your focus as a committee will be on properly recognising the exceptional work of your invaluable team. However, there may be instances that require this process.

The PURPOSE of volunteers is to support the Project and your service users appropriately, as part of a team; they should be an asset. But sometimes volunteers can become a liability. Having a disciplinary and dismissal process for volunteers is vital to ensure that any issues are dealt with quickly and appropriately in order to: ensure the continued smooth-running of your Project; prevent the loss of other volunteers who have been adversely affected by the volunteer's actions or behaviour; protect your service users; safeguard the reputation of your Project; and to protect the limited time of your Volunteering Lead. The disciplinary and dismissal process should form part of your Volunteering Policy – having a 'stand' on it upfront will make it more straightforward if you do need to ask a volunteer to leave – and it should be applied to any and all volunteers, whatever their history with the Project.

Firstly, record the comments and complaints of everyone who witnessed the behaviour, action or incident – in the witness's own words as far as possible, to prevent misunderstandings /

miscommunication. Clarify any colloquialisms – you'll need to check what the witness understands by any unusual words they use. And, if possible / applicable, try to ensure that a member of the committee witnesses the behaviour too: if it's on-going, the more witnesses you have, the better.

As mentioned previously in this chapter, less serious issues – such as turning up very late as a one-off, or failing to turn up once with insufficient notice – would probably be dealt with at the Volunteering Lead's next one-to-one supervision session with the volunteer – and, as long as it doesn't happen again, then it doesn't matter! For more serious performance issues, such as shoddy work, rudeness to other volunteers or to service users, working with no regard for their own safety or the safety of others etc., or for minor issues that are on-going despite attempts to work through them with the volunteer during your supervision sessions, address it; it's not going to go away. Arrange a meeting with the volunteer. Have another member of the committee present as a witness. Prepare what you want to say in advance – write it down to ensure that you don't miss out anything vital, or lose your thread in the meeting. Provide a clear account for the volunteer of 'the issues, the problems they cause and what needs to change'[3]. Find out what the volunteer's perspective is about the issue(s) under discussion, and whether they accept that their actions were unacceptable. If they do recognise this – and as long as they haven't done something that's unforgivable or illegal – devise a plan together and a timescale for improvement. Make sure that this is adhered to, and that the volunteer understands that if they don't follow the plan they will be asked to leave[3]. However, if a volunteer does not accept any responsibility for their behaviour, actions or performance, that leaves you with no constructive way to resolve it to the satisfaction of the team, and you'd have no choice but to ask them to leave. This is because the behaviour, if it's not recognised as inappropriate by the person displaying it, will continue and may escalate.

However, some actions, such as physical violence or verbal abuse, are so serious that they should result in immediate suspension while your Volunteering Lead investigates the incident, and, depending on that outcome, in dismissal. It's never an easy task to dismiss a volunteer, but you need to think about the reputation and long-term health and sustainability of the Project, your service users, and the retention of your other volunteers.

Your Dismissal Process: your Volunteering Lead will have documented each incident, and the comments of everyone who witnessed or were involved in these incidents, with the dates and times. The Lead will have recorded the conversations they will have had with the volunteer about the behaviour / issue, and will have a copy of any Improvement Plans in place etc. When the volunteer's actions have reached the stage where you feel that their behaviour needs to be addressed more formally, the Lead should arrange to meet with them in the presence of another person from your committee – to protect yourselves from any false claims. Or if your Lead is phoning the person (perhaps because they won't come in to meet face-to-face, or because none of you would feel safe if they did) let them know that this person is also present and that the phone is 'on speaker'. Explain that the volunteer will no longer be able to work with the Project in any capacity, and why. Be very clear, revisiting the recorded incidents, the steps necessary / time taken to, for example, cover their work or smooth over their disruption, and reminding the volunteer of the opportunities that they've been given to change their behaviour / stop the action causing issues etc. Don't leave any loopholes, or feel so awkward that you concede you'll give them another chance, either now or in six months' time. Make it a clean break. Do make it all about the incidents / actions that you've reminded them of though, rather than making it about the person themselves. Treat them as you would like to be treated in that situation – i.e. professionally[2]. And end by thanking them for their contribution to the organisation, if it is possible to do this with absolutely no discernible sense of irony.

Corporate Social Responsibility (CSR)

For our purposes, this is the requirement that companies make a positive difference in the community within which they're based. This could be in any number of ways, depending on the resources of the company and their level of commitment – i.e. whether or not they're just 'ticking a box'. It will likely begin (and may end) with a one-off volunteering opportunity for a number of the company's staff. It *could* lead to donations of money as well as offers of equipment etc., and may result in attracting longer term volunteers from within the company's staff team.

Whether your Project's corporate volunteers add value depends to a large extent on the motivation of the company concerned and of their employees, the notice they are able to give you before their volunteering session, and how defined the possible tasks that you identify for them are. Some will, for example, pay their staff to devote a day to a community initiative once a year, or give their staff time regularly in the working week to volunteer locally.

Whatever the allocation of time donated, any collaboration will ideally be the result of a number of conversations between your group and the company's CSR representative, rather than a harassed member of their staff desperately phoning around because this has been no one person's responsibility and the clock's ticking. If it is the latter, though, probably all you'll be able to do is point them towards a practical task that no-one has yet had time to do, and which requires neither supervision nor a DBS check, such as painting a room. And if it's just going to be a waste of your time, you *might* just want to politely look that particular gift horse in the mouth! But a company's willing help *could* be invaluable – e.g. their staff time could be spent helping you to promote your Project through social media etc. With sufficient notice, you could learn the particular strengths of the company and the skills of its employees, and work with them to find a way that staff could add value to your Project in a way that will be engaging for them.

A stipulation for the entire volunteering team: never give advice to service users

Signposting your service users to additional services that could be of benefit to them is to be lauded. But DON'T ever give advice to service users – even if you feel qualified to give it. Your advice probably won't be taken anyway, but that's not the point. You need to provide information, and highlight any choices open to them, objectively, based on their needs and their circumstances as they have related them to you, then step back and let them decide. This will help them to make their own decisions, rather than you making a decision for them, which can only end in tears.

> *For example: I was studying for a counselling qualification and, naturally, as students we weren't let loose to practise our counselling skills on people outside the class, but instead practised on each other. One woman that I was paired with, Sue, was trying to choose between two men. I had a personal opinion, naturally – in fact 'frying pan and fire' sprang to mind – but I didn't express it. Instead I gave Sue the space to talk, and to think out loud. I just reflected back what Sue had told me, and only asked questions that allowed her to clarify her thinking to herself. She chose the man that her family and friends had been most vocal in their disapproval of, but 'the heart wants what the heart wants'.*

Try very hard not to get personally involved, because remaining objective is the best way to help all your service users, and to protect yourself. It's easier said than done – I'm still struggling with it after nearly forty years; you'll empathise with many of the people that you'll be trying to help, especially when you understand their life stories – and if you have a religious faith you might find yourself thinking 'there but for the grace of God...' But it's not going to help anyone if you fall weeping unrestrainedly on the necks of people accessing your service. What will help them is your own objectivity. And you can take comfort in knowing that you are helping that person, and easing their burden a little.

JO'S STORY:

MID-JULY:

With funding confirmed, the committee began the search for volunteers and, in addition to the avenues that they had already identified, Jo contacted Pavel to register the volunteering opportunities with Tall Town CVS. The committee members were DBS checked, and had food safety training, to ensure that the Project's services could be delivered as planned even if there was a delay to either recruiting, checking or training sufficient local volunteers.

ENDNOTES

1. https://mediatrust.org/

2. 'The complete idiot's guide to Recruiting and Managing Volunteers' by USA-based John L. Lipp (2009) pub. By Alpha – a member of Penguin Group (USA) Inc.

3. Voluntary Action Leicestershire – https://valonline.org.uk/

11

ATTRACTING SERVICE USERS: HOW TO ATTRACT PEOPLE WHO COULD BENEFIT FROM YOUR PROJECT

Where will you look?

The work that you've already done in developing relationships with relevant groups and organisations will be absolutely crucial in promoting your Project among potential service users. And this is particularly so with individuals isolated from their communities, such as, for example, rough sleepers and the vulnerably housed, and many older people. These are the same potential service users – along with some families – who may have no access to digital media, and who may need to hear about your service though local organisations first. Additionally, your meeting with the local community (chapter 8) is likely to have provided a source of service users for your Project, either directly or indirectly. And the media and other contacts that you made while promoting that event will serve you well again too. I've also listed further avenues for finding your service users, below. For these it'd be the same process as that outlined in the chapter on Communication (chapter 5) i.e. phone, email, text, speak, repeat.

The CVS or Council's Directory of Services may now be an additional source of service users to your Project: many of the groups listed – which could not have helped you initially with information, support, introductions or resources – may well know of people who could benefit from your Project.

You could contact the local **Council's Health and Wellbeing Board** (via the relevant Councillors / Admin support associated with this Board on the Council's website). This body is made up of representatives from the Council, the Third Sector, the NHS, Public Health, HealthWatch, the Police and Fire Services and sometimes a social housing provider. They have a phenomenal network of providers from every sector, and will be interested in understanding how your Project could help the people they support. Outline your Project – touching upon the relationships you've established within the local Third Sector etc. – and ask that the Project information be disseminated throughout the Board members. If you do get a response, it will most likely be encouragement and a request to keep them in the loop, but it could be more wide-ranging: for example, if they are really interested – and perhaps if it helps to address a current focus for the Council – they make ask to meet you, and / or ask you to present some brief information to the Board about the Project.

Your **Ward councillors** could help with advertising your service and attracting clients.

If you can gain the interest and support of your **local GP Surgery**, they may feel that your Project would be a suitable outlet to recommend to some of their patients – either as a volunteer or service user. Approach the Patient Participation Group (PPG) attached to the practice. This will include GP Practice staff.

There are NHS-funded **Social Prescribers**, recruited in recognition that a person's health and wellbeing is affected by social and economic factors. Your GP Surgery (or local HealthWatch – see below) should be able to give you contact details.

HealthWatch is an independent statutory body, with over 150 offices across England. They could promote your Project in their local newsletter and feature you on their social media site, reaching GPs and hospitals, dentists, pharmacies etc. Just carry out an internet search for 'HealthWatch [town / city]' for their local details, or look at their main website[1].

Faith groups are potentially a source of referrals, as they will know of people within the area who could benefit from your service.

'Places of Welcome' – This is a growing network of local community groups providing a warm welcome every week to anyone who wants to enjoy the company of others. Their service users may become yours too, and vice versa.

Your **volunteers' local knowledge** will be invaluable here too as, depending on the Project, they will be able to give leaflets to, for example, their local hostels for the homeless, their children's schools etc.

Libraries – Library staff will no doubt display a leaflet for you, and may also promote the Project to customers who might benefit from your service – whether that's young families, older people, homeless people…

Warm Spaces – Many faith groups and community centres have been among those providing a warm place for people struggling with the cost of heating their homes. These will be listed on the local Council's website, and could be a further source of service users for your Project.

The Charity Commission – You could search for groups with charitable status by location on the Charity Commission's website. It's a little laborious, but once you skip over the surprising number of scout groups it's not too bad.

I haven't included your **local Social Services Department** for a number of reasons: they are really more focused on crisis management, and would anyway be too cautious to distribute your information to vulnerable clients (and what could be litigation-happy relatives), and naturally would not be permitted to pass on the contact details of their clients to you.

What will you write in your promotion of your Project?

Before you begin to promote your Project's opening, make sure that the opening date and time is confirmed. As with the promotion of the event with the Community (chapter 8), give yourself about six weeks between the start of this promotion and the launch – to allow you to feature in local monthly newsletters etc. You'll want an eye-catching headline and then a very brief outline of the Project: who you want to attract; what the Project actually does / provides; where it'll run from (with directions); when; and how people access it (i.e. do people just turn up, or is there a referral or booking system?) Add the Project's contact details for enquirers.

Don't worry that you'll be overwhelmed by numbers of service users for your first few sessions – that's almost unheard of. It takes time for word to spread, and the proportion of initial 'hits' you get will be low. Don't be disheartened with an initial low turnout: organisations will inevitably be a little too cautious about referrals while they judge your capacity and the take-up of your service etc. This is partly because you've done such a good job in identifying a niche and plugging the gap in provision, that they'll worry your Project will be overwhelmed with interest. *This is something that I found consistently in my work with an older persons' charity: there were just ten places for lonely older people in each small local group (because the get-togethers were held in average-sized family homes) and yet the groups always ran with very low numbers initially because everyone assumed we'd be so oversubscribed that it wasn't worth mentioning to their clients.*

Also you need to build upon the trust you've established with your potential referrers, demonstrating that you're there for the long term by consistently delivering your Project well, monitoring and evaluating the service (see chapter 12) etc. Don't be afraid to cast your net wide either – in some areas service users will travel for miles to get to a worthwhile Project.

JO'S STORY:

MID-JULY:

Now that the committee had received offers of funding for the first year of their Project, they began to promote it widely. The committee's Communications Lead devised a colourful A5-sized leaflet, which outlined the Project at a glance, along with the start date, and included the committee's preferred contact details. There was an electronic version, and the committee had 1000 hard copies printed for dissemination too. Jo revisited all her initial contacts, both to update them as to the good news, and to ask that they help to disseminate this information among their own contacts and (where appropriate) among their service users. Pavel from Community Action agreed to disseminate this information across all the groups and organisations operating within the town in their next monthly newsletter, and promised to circulate the e-leaflet as an attachment accompanying this.

Amy from the Housing Association asked for 100 leaflets to display in the Housing Association's offices, and said that she would also spread the word among their local residents in their next monthly newsletter – both about the free communal meals' service and the volunteering opportunities – and would also disseminate the e-leaflet across the Food Insecurity Network that she facilitated.

Jo contacted Sarah again from 'Families Support in the Sunvale Borough', and Sarah was happy to disseminate information about the impending Project launch to those families in Tall Town known to her, through their monthly newsletter. She also kindly offered to disseminate it through her relevant contacts serving the town, and Jo knew that while a great many of these would already know of the Project, some would not. She gratefully accepted. Jo contacted Beth from the local charity supporting refugees again too, and Beth was really pleased that Jo had been successful in bringing this vital resource to the town. She asked for fifty leaflets, and said that they would also translate it into the languages most commonly used by the families that they supported.

Sunil from Love Tall Town was helpful too with disseminating information, and Clive from the food bank asked for 100 leaflets that he could put in the bags of food collected by his customers.

Parminder from Public Health was pleased to disseminate the Project information among the relevant Trulegate-based services known to herself and her colleagues, using the e-leaflet, and said that she'd also like to pop along to help out as a volunteer.

Jo revisited all the not-for-profit food providers that she had already reached out to, not just the 35% who had already kindly responded (though she expressed her gratitude specifically in the communications to those). She also contacted Matt from the Foodbank Network, and he kindly disseminated the information too. Many who had not had the time or will to respond when the Project was not yet established did reply positively to the news of the Project launch, and those in and around Trulegate requested leaflets so that they could promote it to their service users.

In addition, the committee members and additional volunteers recruited from the Community contacted many local organisations to ask for permission to display leaflets, including: the library; family-friendly fast food outlets; GP surgeries; faith-based and other groups running 'parent and toddler' get-togethers, play groups, scout groups etc; coffee shops; and schools and nurseries. And Jo contacted local representatives of the government initiative Sure Start, Trulegate Ward councillors, the Council's Early Years Officer, and the Council's Trulegate Neighbourhood Office. The Communications Lead reached out to all media sources, including the local neighbourhood website.

ENDNOTES

1. healthwatch.co.uk

12

ENSURING SUSTAINABILITY: MONITORING AND EVALUATION, AND COMMUNICATION

N ow for the best bit – you get to start making a difference. You have your committee in place, and enough volunteers to run your service while you become established and word spreads of the great volunteering opportunities that your Project offers. Your venue is suitable for your Project's needs, and accessible by your service users, the majority of whom will have had a reasonable chance of hearing about your Project. All relevant local groups and organisations are aware of what you'll be providing, and sufficient of them are keen to work in a mutually beneficial way with you. The opening date and running times have been advertised widely. Any equipment or resources that you need are in place, and any remaining funds that were donated are in the Project's bank account. You have secured suitable insurance. Time to cut that ribbon!

No doubt you'll want your Project to last for as long as there's a need for it within your community. The sustainability of your Project will ultimately depend almost entirely on carrying out good monitoring and evaluation, which is effectively communicated, and – crucially – acting on the findings. ('Monitoring' is the ongoing collection and recording of information, and 'Evaluation' is the periodic assessment of that information.) Initially, monitoring and evaluation will indicate the progress that your Project is making towards achieving your Project's objectives, and whether that progress is within the realistic timeframe that you've stipulated to your funders. It will also highlight any problems that need to be addressed, such as dissatisfaction among your volunteers or service users, and the reasons for this. As your Project becomes more established though, acting on the results of monitoring and evaluation will also ensure that the Project doesn't stagnate, relying on outdated information and delivering services that no longer engage volunteers or service users. It will provide the information needed for your Project to continue to be **demonstrably** relevant to your service users, in sufficient numbers to be cost-effective – e.g. it'll cost the same to keep the lights on for twenty people as for one. And your Project will be able to evolve and adapt, ensuring that it is always delivered in a way that will encourage service users to utilise your service, volunteers to support it, and relevant organisations to signpost people to it.

You'll need to think about:

- the information that will demonstrate how you are achieving your Project's objectives

- how you are going to collect and record it effectively

- how you are going to act on your committee's subsequent evaluation of it.

In terms of the questions that you ask, keep it simple: just the information that you absolutely need for the Project to run effectively and to continue to be relevant to service users and supported by volunteers. You'll need to explain the reasons for these questions to your survey participants, and assure people that their responses will be anonymous (see chapter 9 on 'Data Protection').

How are you going to find out the answers to your questions?

You'll need to decide: who'll be collecting the information, what form(s) the research will take, how often it'll be collected, and who is going to collate and interpret it. Volunteers will be able to gather a great deal of day-to-day information for you – such as a headcount for each session, the number of people that volunteers gave information to, and how many were signposted on (and to which organisations) etc.

Your research questions will probably be answered through a mix of (targeted) conversation (i.e. a chat during which you find out the answers to a few key questions) and 'participant observation' (i.e. looking around to check that people seem to be engaged with tasks or conversation, and not sitting alone when they don't want to be). It might be that periodic surveys are appropriate too. We touched upon them in chapter 2, and there's more in-depth information below. You will also want to hear from your volunteers, and from the organisations that signposted service users to you, about how they perceive the Project is progressing (the latter will have heard comments from the service users that they signposted to you). And you'll want to learn what suggestions volunteers, service users and referrers might have to strengthen and possibly expand the service. Utilise whatever research methods work best for you and the team, and use them in combination if that's appropriate – from regular informal chats and occasional brief surveys, to meetings when you present information briefly, answer any questions and invite feedback and suggestions.

'Quantitative' and 'Qualitative' information

Gather a mix of 'quantitative' information (i.e. *quantifiable* or measurable, such as the number of attendees, or the number of meals served etc) and 'qualitative' information (comments, suggestions etc). Together, both types of information will be useful measures for you to judge where you are in relation to your Project's objectives, i.e. the qualitative answers that you get as a result of targeted conversations and surveys are going to be useful to interpret the quantitative statistics that you've collected – e.g. to learn why numbers of attendees are growing so quickly or slowing down.

Quantitative information – Measurable (quantifiable) information includes:

- **Where did attendees hear about you?** This will tell you where your promotion of this Project has been most effective, and which local organisations are signposting their service users to you.

- **How many people are attending each week?** Is the number growing, and approaching the 'target' number that you gave to funders and other supporters?

- **Are the same people coming along each week?** This implies that you're doing something right! But it might be that not enough people are learning about it. Again, revisit your promotional avenues, and try to identify others. And ask your service users if they will promote it by word of mouth.

- **Do some attendees come along once and not return?** You'd want to know why, by talking with the volunteers and other service users that had spoken with the person, and, if they had given you permission to contact them, by asking them directly why they decided not to return, if that is appropriate for your service users. There could be any number of reasons, many of which are fixable: sometimes it's a personality clash among some group members, or that your service didn't give them enough time just to chat between the activities...

- **What local areas are your service users traveling from? And how are they getting there?** Is transport a problem within those areas – and, crucially, within the local areas not well represented by your service users – either because of availability, cost, or proximity of e.g. the bus stop to your venue?

- **What other groups do your service users attend during the month?** You could contact those group organisers and ask that they highlight the Project. They will get points for signposting.

Qualitative information – Qualitative information will allow you to properly gauge whether the aims of your Project are being met: how much your service users enjoy the sessions; whether they feel welcomed, less lonely, valued, respected, etc. Qualitative questions directed at service users should be brief, to the point and probably administered not more than once every three or four months initially (then annually or bi-annually after the first year). Qualitative information is great for quotes and (with the permission and involvement of the service user) for case studies. Both quotes and case studies should be anonymised, removing all identifying information, to protect the service user who is taking part. You'll have read case studies – an outline of the person's life and the challenges they have encountered and continue to face, and how this Project is making a difference to them, and in what way. Like positive quotes, case studies are also very motivating for volunteers (and indeed for paid staff), so share them widely. They are also very useful to communicate the positive impact of your project on the lives of your service users to your current and future funders.

> *For example: when talking to funders about the need to support the work of the older persons' charity that I worked for at the time, I would tell them of one older lady who, before joining the charity's free service, had been so lonely and isolated that the only way she*

could mark the passing weeks was to sit in an armchair during the week and on the settee at weekends.

Take a moment to think about that. It'll probably stay with you.

Typical qualitative questions would include:

- **What do attendees think of the venue / timing of the get-together / atmosphere / activities?**

- **What is the Project doing right?!**

- **What suggestions do attendees have to improve existing services? And to increase the range and scope of the service?** If your service users feel some 'ownership' of the Project they are more likely to participate fully

- **What do the service users themselves hope to gain from your Project?** This feedback will help to guide your current provision and also your growth as the Project evolves

- **Ultimately, have you met the aims of your Project?** For example, if your service users are isolated older people, do they feel less lonely as a result of attending the weekly get-togethers? Have they made friends? etc.

Remember to keep it simple from the start. And the results aren't an end in themselves, but instead provide the information that will enable you and your committee to identify and address any problems or issues, and to grow as a service in the direction that is most helpful for your service users, and delivered in the way that is supported by your volunteers.

Just a note here on growing your service: any sustainable growth must certainly be led by the needs of your service users within the local community, as identified through your multifaceted research. But, equally, it should take into account both of the factors that underpin a great Project: good people and sufficient resources.

You would need both for any sustained growth and, even with these in excess, you need to pace yourselves. I suppose, in the end, a sustainable Project embodies Aesop's fable of the Hare and the Tortoise: doing things steadily and at a considered pace will be more successful over the longer term than acting quickly and rashly.

Maintaining momentum through communication

The person collating and interpreting (evaluating) the findings of the monitoring that is carried out will need to communicate the results to the committee. And then you'll all need to decide what actions (if any) you need to take for your Project to continue to be relevant and useful. And throughout the duration of your Project you'll want to continue to keep the service users, volunteers, relevant local groups and organisations, funders and the wider community in the loop – and the more you adhere to this the longer your Project will last. So, provide periodic updates, cut and pasted into *personalised* emails. One or two pages will do it – colourful and informative, with some useful statistics, case studies and quotes from satisfied service users and from referring organisations and volunteers. The benefits of this will be far-reaching: you will maintain the hard-won relationships that you've established; ensure a steady flow of referrals to your Project; and when you have reached capacity you can let your referrers know that you'll subsequently be maintaining a waiting list (if that's appropriate to your service); and be able to signpost service users appropriately to further sources of support; you will have relevant community groups to partner with for funding bids; and you will be able to share in any resources that are provided by the Council to relevant local services, as well as the (often relatively random) resources that some businesses kindly donate in bulk – e.g. multiple boxes of chocolates, plimsolls, Easter eggs, candles – that another organisation may be offered but which they are unable to use themselves.

Fixing Problems

Problems can arise, of any size, no matter how well you plan. Sometimes things just happen, in the same way that toast can fall butter-side down. But don't worry – remember that with all the good work you've done, all the planning and all the safeguards that you've built in with your policies and insurance, and with the mutually beneficial relationships that you've established with local individuals, groups and organisations, any problem is extremely unlikely to be a blow to your plans. If a problem does arise, the first thing to do is to identify exactly what the problem or issue is, as it arises. Is it a fundamental one, or a 'quick fix'? Whichever it is, don't ignore it, because it won't go away. Instead treat it as a chance to make your Project even better, and even more sustainable: glass half full stuff. So now – listen to the person highlighting the problem, and to those that you'll need to speak with about it. Ask all of these for guidance / advice / next steps / suggestions. You've established a team of people both within your committee and external to it who have invested precious time and resources into this: no-one wants it to fail. And, while it sounds trite, it is true that 'Where there's a will, there's a way.'

JO'S STORY:

The Family Dining Project started at the beginning of September. Jo came across her initial 150 words outline for her proposed Project, and reflected on the learning that had changed and enriched the way the Project would be delivered, while maintaining the core of her vision: helping to enable local families to eat healthily.

Three months after the Family Dining Project opened, the committee members circulated a brief survey to service users, to make sure that the team were serving an appropriate menu, in the right atmosphere, and in a way that made everyone feel warmly welcomed and comfortable. The feedback was very pleasing, and any negative comments were around practicalities such as not having somewhere to hang coats, which were easily rectified. The positive feedback formed the basis of the

Communication Lead's first quarterly Family Dining Project newsletter, and – as with all subsequent newsletters – it was circulated (predominantly in an electronic version) to service users, volunteers, funders, and all organisations and local groups that were relevant to the Project, either in terms of not-for-profit food provision or the support of local families.

Six months after opening a further survey was circulated to both service users and volunteers, for suggestions for improving and / or expanding the existing service, and for other services that could be run alongside this one. (It was explained that funding applications would need to be submitted at this stage to support the Project's work after the first year, so that the committee needed to learn the impact of the Project on local families, and find out whether there was scope for improvement and / or expansion of the service. Everyone was promised that any subsequent survey would be annual or bi-annual, and was assured that the committee members would warmly welcome comments and suggestions at any time from both service users and volunteers.) Among the suggestions resulting from this second survey were: a toy library, a clothes bank specifically for outfits suitable for job interviews, and a selection of books written for adults who were learning English as an additional language. Cooking classes had been suggested too, but another organisation was already delivering these locally and the committee made sure that interested service users and volunteers were signposted to this. Several volunteers asked that food safety training be available to all volunteers rather than solely to lead volunteers, and First Aid training too. Two volunteers asked whether there was a possibility that they might be able to undergo Active Listening training.

In addition to working to attract funding to maintain the Project's existing service, the committee needed to discuss any plans for expansion, and the implications of implementing changes such as hiring a suitable food storage facility nearby, so that they could cut costs by bulk-buying surplus food. They also needed to speak about the training requests from volunteers, as well as researching and considering the suggestions made by service users and volunteers for any additional services.

13

CONCLUSION

T he work that you're doing and that is ahead of you to set up and run your Project is all going to be worthwhile. You're taking steps to make a positive difference within your community, joining others who are already working to make that change within their own communities. Like them, you'll be helping people who you probably don't know, but who are in need, who are struggling or vulnerable or hungry or isolated. No act of kindness or compassion is ever wasted.

I need to share something with you now that has been hard-won: you can't save everyone or solve everything, and you must not expect that of yourself. But you and your team can be a key piece in the jigsaw, playing your part in easing some truly dreadful burdens, and you should be proud of that, and content. I once worked for a charity whose volunteers each spent a few hours once a month driving lonely older people to tea parties hosted by other volunteers in their own homes, where the guests enjoyed afternoon tea together in good company. It might sound like a 'drop in the ocean', but when someone marks the passing of time by sitting on a settee at weekends and an armchair during the week, those few hours in the month are a treasured lifeline. And I remember that, at the funeral of one of the charity's older guests, her daughter said that the group had given her Mum three more years of happiness towards the end of her life. What I'm trying to say is that while you cannot expect to be the whole answer, don't underestimate the difference that you'll make. So:

> 'Start where you are. Use what you have.
> Do what you can.'[1]

ENDNOTES

1. Arthur Ashe on Volunteering.

APPENDICES

A: JO'S PRESENTATION TO LOCAL ORGANISATIONS
(near the beginning of her research and networking)

Slide 1:

The Family Dining Charity

(Charity registration number ----------)

JO SAYS: Hi. My name is Jo Stead, and I'm the Chair of the Family Dining Charity. I'd like to begin by thanking Amy for the opportunity to meet with you all today, and to introduce this charity to you. Over the next five minutes I'm just going to briefly outline the aims of the charity, and our vision for supporting the families that are struggling to source healthy meals in Tall Town. At the end of that time I'll be keen to answer any questions that you might have.

Slide 2: Dining together as a Community

- Free healthy two course meals for the whole family to enjoy, communally

- Twice a week

- Preventing any duplication of existing provision

JO SAYS: We're working to set up a Family Dining Project in Tall Town, providing delicious, hot and nutritious meals for families who are struggling to source healthy food regularly. This is going to be a completely free service, and a communal activity, enabling local families to meet together and enjoy each other's company over a hearty two course meal twice a week.

My initial research would suggest that there is currently no similar service running within any area of Tall Town, but to ensure that we're not just duplicating existing services, I really need to find out exactly what is currently being offered, and where. You're the experts here and I would welcome the opportunity to speak with you all individually, to find out about the services that you provide in more depth. I'd also welcome introductions to any and all relevant local groups and organisations. My contacts details will be on the final slide here – and Amy has them too. Please do get in touch.

Slide 3: What our initial research has indicated

- Three areas of high deprivation within the town:

    - Biddlevale
    - Tymbown
    - Trulegate

JO SAYS: As you'll know, these are all areas of high deprivation within Tall Town, across all seven measures. And of course these all score highly for Income Deprivation affecting Children too. These areas are currently the focus of our work in the town.

Slide 4: Who we've spoken with so far

The local organisations and groups that we've contacted so far:

- Tall Town CVS (Pavel)
- Tall Town Independent Foodbank (Clive)
- Love Tall Town
- All not-for-profit food providers listed on the Council's Directory.

Networks:

- Tall Town's Foodbank Network (Matt)
- And this Food Insecurity Network (Amy).

JO SAYS: These are the groups and organisations that we've reached out to so far, and additionally the two networks who have been so kind and welcoming. Clive has given us an overview of not-for-profit food provision in the town, and of course Amy very kindly invited me to speak with you today. I'm waiting to hear back from Love Tall Town and the majority of not-for-profit food providers, but it's early days.

Slide 5: Funding

- Where's the money coming from?

JO SAYS: We've identified several potential funders who are keen to fund community-led support for local people and, as soon as we have identified an area of unmet need within the town, with the facilities we need, we'll be submitting funding applications.

Slide 6: Contact Details

Names / Roles of the Chair, Treasurer, Secretary and
Communications Lead.

The charity's:

Email address: _____

Facebook page: _____

Mobile phone number: _____

(registered charity number _____

Any Questions?

> **JO SAYS:** Here's one final slide, giving our contact details,
> and registered charity number. And now, do you have any
> questions or comments?

After answering any questions, Jo ended by repeating her request
for people to contact her with information on their organisation's
services, and with any other guidance and advice.

_____

_____

B: JO'S PRESENTATION TO LOCAL GROUPS AND ORGANISATIONS
(when the Project concept is fully formed)

Slide I:

The Family Dining Charity
(Charity registration number -----------)

JO SAYS: Hi. My name is Jo Stead, and I'm the Chair of the Family Dining Charity. Over the next five minutes I'm just going to briefly explain the aims of the charity, and how we see this working in Trulegate. At the end of that time I'll be keen to answer any questions that you might have.

Slide 2: Dining together as a Community in Trulegate

- Free two course meals for the whole family to enjoy

- Twice a week – Mondays and Thursdays

- Vegetarian menu

JO SAYS: We're working to set up a Family Dining Project in Trulegate, providing delicious, hot and nutritious meals for families living locally who are struggling to source healthy food regularly. This is going to be a completely free service – and a good opportunity for local families to be able to meet together and enjoy each other's company over a hearty two course meal.

We are planning to provide the communal meals from the Trulegate Community Centre on a Monday and a Thursday every week, beginning service at 5.30 p.m.

The meals will be vegetarian, predominantly to make them more inclusive, but also because it'll be much more straight-forward to adhere to food safety requirements as we're not including meat and fish.

Slide 3: Why we chose Trulegate

- An area of high deprivation

- A strong sense of community

- Suitable local venue

JO SAYS: As to why we chose Trulegate – firstly, as you'll know, Trulegate is an area of high deprivation within Tall Town, across all seven measures, and additionally it scores highly for Income Deprivation affecting Children. And, while the same could be said for Tymbown and Biddlevale, we were also looking for an area that has a cohesive community, where everyone will pull together and go out of their way to help each other, because this Project will be very much supported by local volunteers. Our conversations with community-based groups and organisations such as yourselves, and with representatives from the local council, have all pointed us towards Trulegate as the ideal location. We also needed an area with a suitable local venue – with a semi-commercial kitchen and dining for thirty plus people, within walking distance of as many local families who could benefit from this free service as possible. The Trulegate Community Centre is ideal, being well utilised by the residents of the surrounding social housing estate.

Slide 4: The Practicalities

- Meals cooked at the venue by volunteers

- Every ingredient listed

- Fruit.

JO SAYS: *All the meals will be cooked in the venue's kitchen, from scratch, using only fresh ingredients. We'll be subscribing to twice-weekly deliveries of fresh surplus food from [name of the Borough's distributor].*

Just in case of allergies, every ingredient for both dishes will be listed on a chalk board in the dining room. If any meals include ingredients from a packet or tin, for example custard powder or gravy, the brand will also be specified, and the list of ingredients making up this pre-prepared foodstuff available for anyone to read.

We'll also try to source a good selection of fruit as an alternative or addition to the dessert provided.

Slide 5: Who we've spoken with so far

The local organisations and groups that we've spoken with:

- Tall Town CVS (Pavel)
- Tall Town Independent Foodbank (Clive)
- Sunvale Housing Association (Amy)
- Love Tall Town (Sunil)
- The Council's Public Health department (Parminder)
- All not-for-profit food providers in the town, including Trulegate's 'pay what you can' community café
- Beacon of Hope in Tall Town (Beth)
- Families Support in the Sunvale Borough (Sarah)

Networks:

- Tall Town's Foodbank Network (Matt)
- And the local Food Insecurity Network (Amy).

JO SAYS: These are the groups and organisations that we've spoken with so far – and I see many of you here this morning – Hi again! The final two are the networks that have kindly and warmly welcomed us. Everyone has been hugely supportive and helpful. Just to briefly pick out two or three: Clive gave us the picture of not-for-profit food provision in the town, and Beth from Beacon of Hope first got us thinking about the benefits of a vegetarian menu. The manager of the community café, Tom, suggested that volunteers from the community would be attracted by being able to dine too, both for the healthy food and for the social side of eating together. I feel that it's been a really cooperative and supportive process, and a very productive one.

Slide 6: Next steps

- Funding
- Signposting.

JO SAYS: You may be wondering where the money is coming from! We've submitted fund-raising bids to seven potential funders, all of whom have responded positively to our applications. We'll know exactly how much we'll be getting, and from which funders, by mid-July at the latest. The plan is to begin the family dining get-togethers in early September.

We'll keep you in the loop of course, and will be more than happy to signpost the families that we'll be supporting to any of your services that are relevant to them. We'll be asking that you do the same, of course.

Slide 7: Contact Details

The Family Dining Charity: free communal meals for the families of Trulegate

Names / Roles of the Chair, Treasurer, Secretary and Communications Lead.

The charity's:

Email address: _____

Facebook page: _____

Mobile phone number: _____

(registered charity number _____

Any Questions?

> **JO SAYS:** *Here's one final slide, giving our contact details, and registered charity number. And now, do you have any questions or comments?*

_____

_____

C: JO'S PRESENTATION TO THE LOCAL COMMUNITY

Slide 1:

The Family Dining Project

(Charity registration number-------)

JO SAYS: Hi. My name is Jo Stead, and I'm the Chair of the Family Dining Project. Over the next five minutes I'm just going to briefly explain the Project itself, and how we see this working in Trulegate. If you could wait until the end of these few slides before you ask any questions I'd appreciate that, as the answer to your question may be covered within this presentation.

Slide 2: Dining together as a Community in Trulegate

- Free two course meals for the whole family to enjoy, communally

- Twice a week – Mondays and Thursdays.

   JO SAYS: So, we're working to set up a Family Dining Project in Trulegate. This is going to be a completely free service – and a good opportunity for local families to be able to meet together and enjoy each other's company over a delicious, hot and healthy two course meal. We are planning to provide the communal meals from this Centre on a Monday and a Thursday every week, beginning service at 5.30p.m.

Slide 3: Why we chose Trulegate

- Trulegate has a strong sense of Community

- Easy to access venue.

   JO SAYS: Firstly, we were looking for an area that has a cohesive community, where everyone will pull together and go out of their way to help each other – because this Project will be very much supported by volunteers from within the local Community. Every organisation that we've spoken with, and the views of those of our committee members living in this area, pointed us towards Trulegate as the ideal location.

   We also needed an area with a suitable local venue, with a decent-sized kitchen and dining area, and if possible located within walking distance of as many local families who could benefit from this free service as possible. This Community Centre is ideal.

Slide 4: The Practicalities

- Meals cooked at the venue by volunteers

- Every ingredient listed

- Fruit.

  NOTES: All the meals will be cooked in the venue's kitchen, from scratch, using only fresh ingredients. We'll be getting a twice-weekly delivery of fresh surplus food from [name the Borough's distributor], but if you know of anyone with an allotment, or who runs an independent grocery store, we'd love to be able to supplement these deliveries with local produce.

  Just in case of allergies, every ingredient for both dishes will be listed on a chalk board in the dining room.

  We'll also try to source a good selection of fruit as an alternative or addition to the dessert provided.

Slide 5: Who we've spoken with so far

The local organisations and groups that we've spoken with:

- Tall Town CVS

- Tall Town Independent Foodbank

- Sunvale Housing Association

- Love Tall Town

- The Council's Public Health department

- All not-for-profit food providers in the town (including Trulegate's 'pay what you can' community café).

- Beacon of Hope in Tall Town

- Families Support in the Sunvale Borough.

Networks:

- Tall Town's Foodbank Network

- Tall Town's Food Insecurity Network.

  JO SAYS: These are the groups and organisations that we've spoken with so far, and the final two are the networks that we've delivered presentations to. We are confident that nothing like this runs currently in the whole of Tall Town, and there has been a lot of support among local groups and organisations, and the local Council, for this free communal meals service. Everyone felt that Trulegate would be an ideal place for this, as there is a strong sense of community within this Ward – people look out for one another and support each other.

Slide 6: Funding

- Where's the money coming from?

  NOTES: We've submitted fund-raising bids to seven potential funders, all of whom have responded positively to our applications. We'll know exactly how much we'll be getting, and from which funders, by mid-July at the latest. The plan is to begin the family dining get-togethers in early September.

Slide 7: Questions for you!

- Do you think this free communal meals service would have the support of the local community?

- Is this venue easy to get to? On the days and at the times we're envisaging?

- Would you prefer a once a week or twice-weekly meal?

- Would you favour dining together over takeaway meals?

- Do you know of any other similar provision locally?

- Are there any popular events for families or for children already running on a Monday or Thursday evening locally?

- Is 5.30 p.m. a good time to start?

JO SAYS: We'll spend time together as a group looking at all these points this evening. Just picking out the main points for now though, we need to learn from yourselves whether: you like the idea of dining together as a community, and whether the timings suit the vast majority of local families. And we'd also like to hear your comments about the proposed service, and any suggestions that you feel could improve the plan.

Firstly though, our contact details -

Slide 8: Contact Details

Names / Roles of the Chair, Treasurer, Secretary and Communications Lead.

The Project's:

Email address: _____

Facebook page: _____

Mobile phone number: _____

(registered charity number _____

JO SAYS: Right then, this is the final slide – just a note of our contact details. They are also on the leaflets that you'll have seen on the back table. Now, does anyone have any questions that they'd like to ask, before we begin to ask for your input on the points from the previous slide?

Acknowledgements:

First and foremost, I'd like to thank my lovely husband Stephen, who read every draft of this book, and whose many questions ensured that it shows all the working out. I'm also extremely grateful to Angela Richardson, who generously shared her considerable expertise in community-based fundraising with me, providing invaluable help and guidance. And many thanks to Andrea Romero O'Brien for creating the lovely artwork in Chapter 3, to my son Tim Walker for summing up WhatsApp, to Jess Phillimore for explaining online fundraising platforms to me, and to Tom Osborne for all the information on environmental policies. Much gratitude is also due to Peter Korn of Interface Legal Advisory Service (a solicitor recommended by the National Council for Voluntary Organisations) for his indispensable input into Chapter 4, and to Duncan House of Southampton City Mission, and the team at the Swindon Food Collective, for providing illustrative statistics from some of their services.

And not forgetting my dog Barney, for keeping me company during all those early morning writing sessions.